10/10/2022

Dear C[...]

Her[e is my book ...] after wor[king on it ...] 16 months. I feel [good?] that the book came together well and I am excited about it. I like my captive title, and I like how the cover turned out — the design team putting two of Dick's pictures together. I think the children (our grandchildren) look like they are talking and wondering if maybe Mighty angels will descend from the opening in the sky.

It was good visiting with you this past spring & I am glad it worked out that we could meet.

My earnest desire for this book is that it might be helpful to some, may encourage some, might even prick someone's conscience, and maybe even some seeds could be planted in fertile ground. Then all the work will be worthwhile. But it is worthwhile too as sorta my legacy to pass down to my children, grandchildren, and to others!

So enjoy reading it, email me what you think about it, and you will find some stories about you and some of our adventures. How brave we were to make that California trip and back again! And wonderful the worst thing that happened was losing our car-top carrier. Very funny now!

Author
Judith Kuipers Walhout

LITTLE ANGELS
AND
MIGHTY ANGELS

JUDITH KUIPERS WALHOUT

WestBow
PRESS®
A DIVISION OF THOMAS NELSON
& ZONDERVAN

Copyright © 2022 Judith Kuipers Walhout.

All rights reserved. No part of this book may be used or reproduced by any means, graphic, electronic, or mechanical, including photocopying, recording, taping or by any information storage retrieval system without the written permission of the author except in the case of brief quotations embodied in critical articles and reviews.

This book is a work of non-fiction.

I have permission from the family kidnapped in Haiti to tell some of their story in my book. They read over what I wrote and approved it.

Also, I got permission from the people mentioned in the book, to use their first names.

WestBow Press books may be ordered through booksellers or by contacting:

WestBow Press
A Division of Thomas Nelson & Zondervan
1663 Liberty Drive
Bloomington, IN 47403
www.westbowpress.com
844-714-3454

Because of the dynamic nature of the Internet, any web addresses or links contained in this book may have changed since publication and may no longer be valid. The views expressed in this work are solely those of the author and do not necessarily reflect the views of the publisher, and the publisher hereby disclaims any responsibility for them.

Any people depicted in stock imagery provided by Getty Images are models, and such images are being used for illustrative purposes only. Certain stock imagery © Getty Images.

Cover pictures were taken by Richard Walhout

ISBN: 978-1-6642-7479-2 (sc)
ISBN: 978-1-6642-7478-5 (e)

Print information available on the last page.

WestBow Press rev. date: 8/17/2022

All Scripture quotations, unless otherwise indicated, are taken from the Holy Bible, New International Version®, NIV®. Copyright ©1973, 1978, 1984, 2011 by Biblica, Inc.® Used by permission of Zondervan. All rights reserved worldwide. www.zondervan.com The "NIV" and "New International Version" are trademarks registered in the United States Patent and Trademark Office by Biblica, Inc.®

Scripture marked (KJV) taken from the King James Version of the Bible.

Scripture quotations marked (TLB) are taken from The Living Bible, copyright © 1971 by Tyndale House Foundation. Used by permission of Tyndale House Publishers, Carol Stream, Illinois 60188. All rights reserved.

Scripture quotations marked MSG are taken from The Message, copyright © 1993, 2002, 2018 by Eugene H. Peterson. Used by permission of NavPress. All rights reserved. Represented by Tyndale House Publishers.

Scripture quotations marked (NLT) are taken from the Holy Bible, New Living Translation, copyright ©1996, 2004, 2015 by Tyndale House Foundation. Used by permission of Tyndale House Publishers, Carol Stream, Illinois 60188. All rights reserved.

CONTENTS

Preface And Dedication ix

Chapter 1   Twenty Shots, Daring Venture, California 1
Chapter 2   Trip Home, Surprise, New Jobs 17
Chapter 3   Snowmobiling, Marriage, God's Gift 25
Chapter 4   Bus Driving, Winter Mishaps, Retired 31
Chapter 5   Storm, Mexico, Protection 45
Chapter 6   Ice Storm, No Power, Downed Trees 60
Chapter 7   New Era, Child-Rearing, Angels 67
Chapter 8   Long Trip, Snowcoach, Mexico Stories 75
Chapter 9   Fearful Times, Kids' Sayings, Snowmobiling 101
Chapter 10 Busy Days, Family Trip, Beauty of Nature 118
Chapter 11 Family Activities, Bats, Scares 143
Chapter 12 Parents, Early Jobs, Encouragement 167
Chapter 13 Suggestions, Indonesia, Heartaches 186
Chapter 14 Blessings, Grandchildren, David 205
Chapter 15 Angels, Protection, Retirement 218

A Note from the Author 265

PREFACE AND DEDICATION

My very first book, *A Farm Girl's Memories*, was published in the summer of 2020. Many let me know how much they enjoyed the book, and numerous people said I should write a sequel. My initial thoughts were, "No. . . I do not want to go through all that work, and likely face many challenges, frustrations, and obstacles again." My goal of actually writing a book was accomplished, and that should be satisfaction enough. My book made it into the hands of a considerable number of readers . . . more than I ever anticipated! It was extremely amazing the many people who wound up with a copy. I made contacts with people I knew from the past whom I had not been in touch with for years! That was really special! So I was completely satisfied with the outcome of my first book. But thoughts of writing another book would not go away. To be able to communicate to others in a book is very worthwhile to me. One night when reading in a devotional book, again I felt the answer was "Yes, write book number two." Being I felt compelled to do it, I think that was God's answer. I am 77 years old already, and the years are so swiftly ticking by . . . what would I still like to do in life? When I look at it from that perspective, the answer is definitely yes---I would like to write another book!

Once I told a friend I feel I can verbalize myself on paper better sometimes than in live conversation. I like to be able to express things from deep down and put in print what I am thinking. It is good to get my feelings, thoughts, and stories written down in order to share them with others. But more than that, I want the book to honor God, and I pray that I will be led by the Spirit to write things that could help others in their day-to-day living. I want to tell the truth about God, help people grow in Him, and get both believers and nonbelievers thinking about spiritual things.

So these thoughts keep coming to my mind, nudging and prodding me; yes, maybe I can write another book. And the ideas for it begin to trickle in. The catchy title would be *Little Angels and Mighty Angels,* and I could include stories and happenings from where I left off with my first book. You will just have to read the book to see where the angels come in. I do enjoy writing, and that would justify writing another book which takes a LOT of time, hard work, effort, dedication, enthusiasm, and fortitude. I like sharing stories and happenings that have transpired . . . put it in writing for my husband, children, sons-in-law, grandchildren, extended family, and hopefully many others. I once heard someone say, "Everyone has a story to tell." I like that, and I think it is true. Everyone perhaps does not care to tell their story or share it, and that is okay. It is up to each person individually, but I have the time and I do not mind sharing some more of my story. I began my story in *A Farm Girl's Memories,* and I will continue my story in *Little Angels and Mighty Angels.* My first book was dedicated to a good friend, Linda, who had once said that I should write a book. And it was because of that one comment that I finally wrote a book! I also dedicated it to my husband and our four daughters. This second book I would like to dedicate again to my husband, daughters, and also to my four wonderful sons-in-law, and my grandchildren. I may show partiality when it comes to family, but I am very fond of them and feel God has blessed us with a wonderful family! I hope you enjoy the various happenings, events, and stories that I have included in my second book.

My thanks again to those who edited my book---daughter Nichole, sister Darlene, friend Renetta Brovont, and a couple others who preferred to remain anonymous. I could not have done it without them. Their help was invaluable and so appreciated!

My prayer for my book was that God would lay on my heart what to write and that it would be a blessing to many others. I needed His guidance so my thoughts and words would be an inspiration to others and benefit them in some way as they continued daily along life's journey. There was also some spiritual insight included which I hoped would be helpful. It is so important to use every opportunity to tell others about Christ and His love for everyone. I feel strongly my opportunity in my retirement is to be a witness with the words in my book! As for the title, *Little Angels and Mighty Angels* . . . we have angels all around us, even if we do not sense their presence. Psalm 103:20-21 says, "Praise the Lord, you His angels, you MIGHTY ONES [or those who excel in strength] who do His bidding [or commandments], who obey His word. Praise the Lord, all His heavenly hosts, you His servants who do His will."

As a Christian, I believe and hopefully expect powerful, *mighty, guardian angels* to be beside me, watching over me each day, as I travel down the paths of life. Perhaps at the last minute we did not board a bus, get in a taxi, get on a plane, or we took a different road because angels directed us away from major trouble or a serious accident. There may be, however, some instances when a person can sense one of these special heavenly beings intervening in their lives, guarding and protecting. In this book, *Little Angels and Mighty Angels*, you can read of some of those special times when I believe God, through His angels, protected me and my family. My first book was mostly about my younger and teenage years when I was growing up on our small farm. This second book will include what I did after college, married life, some trips, raising a family, and on up to my life now as a 77-year-old. So it is time for you to sit down, relax and put your feet up, and enjoy *Little Angels and Mighty Angels*.

I will conclude here with a verse I love in Psalm 91:11-12, "For He will command His *angels* concerning you to guard you in all your ways; they will lift you up in their hands, so that you will not strike your foot against a stone." What a beautiful, wonderful verse promising us security and protection.

TWENTY SHOTS, DARING VENTURE, CALIFORNIA

"But they that wait upon the Lord shall renew their strength; they shall mount up with wings as eagles; they shall run, and not be weary; and they shall walk, and not faint" (Isaiah 40:31 KJV).

"Judy . . . wake up! Wake up, Judy!" I heard this stern and very commanding voice filled with concern as I tried to wake up out of the fog of unconsciousness and come back to reality. It was hard to fight through the daze and was not easy to wake up . . . I was so very, very tired! I just wanted to sleep and sleep! This was after I had to go back to the labor room for another check up, procedure, and blood transfusions.

The reason I was so exhausted was because of 21 hours of labor and the very difficult birth of our baby girl. For twelve of those hours I was in severe labor pain! My husband was there through a good portion of that time except for a few hours of sleep in the night, and when he went to get something to eat. I do not know how he could stand all that moaning and groaning; it was rough! Finally, the doctor had come in and said I was dilated enough, and I was wheeled into delivery after being there since

7 p.m. the night before. Dr. Johnson needed to use forceps to assist with the birth because our little girl came face first. It took another hour after she was born to finish with everything. I was so very tired from then on. I knew what was going on but I just wanted to sleep!

Later that evening though, I was wheeled back in the labor room for another check up because I was bleeding heavily. More pain, but nothing phased me since I was too sleepy. That was when the doctor was very concerned and was trying to get me to wake up. After that procedure, Dick stayed until a little after 9:30 p.m. and watched while they hooked up blood, then finally left for a well needed night of rest. How thankful I was that he was there with me through it all. I was given two units of blood that night, and they came in every hour all night long to check on me. So, what a delivery for me having lost so much blood! Our daughter was a large baby weighing nine pounds and fourteen and a half ounces. But it was a very close call that night and definitely a time in our lives when we felt God protected us through a very difficult situation. That night I felt a little like the apostle Paul where in Acts 27:23 he said, "For last night an *angel* of the God to whom I belong and whom I serve *stood beside me*." (Liv. NT Bible). And thus a reason for the title of my book, *Little Angels and Mighty Angels*. God's hand was protecting me getting me through that critical time, and perhaps He had sent one of His *mighty angels* into that delivery room with us, saving me to be a mother to my new first baby and a wife to my husband.

After that frightening and traumatic night, I was kept in the hospital for six days. In those days it was common to stay several days after the birth of a baby. Plus, I had quite a time of it, so the doctor wanted to make sure I was completely rested before I was allowed to go home. Dr. Johnson even said I could write a book on my stay in the hospital. If I counted all the pricks (shots) I had that week, you could call me a pin cushion! I was very weak and had an exceptionally fast and fluttering heart rhythm. They gave me an iron shot in the hip to help strengthen my body. I had three shots for pain in the labor room, one poke in the labor room to start an I.V., two or three shots for a local anesthetic, three pricks when trying to start I.V.'s after delivery, two shots at least for blood samples, three for blood tests each morning (plus two more as one nurse tried three times), one shot for my RH negative blood, and one when they started giving me blood, all in all a total of 20 pokes and that is a lot of times to be stuck with needles! But I made it through that hospital stay safely, and I will include some more incidents when I feel God surely was protecting us with His *mighty angels*.

First, I will back up to an interesting and quite unusual trip before I was married. I call it unusual as it was a very venturesome feat for two young ladies 23 and 19 years old to take a trip like we did from Michigan to California all by ourselves! We called this trip a dream come true. I know our folks were very concerned about us young ladies attempting that big trip all on our own, and they tried to talk us out of it, but we had made up our minds to do it. After I had worked for two years in a hospital in Grand Rapids, and my girlfriend, Cam, had gone to college for two years, we stayed with my folks for the summer and worked at a local canning company (where my future husband was the plant manager). We needed to save up extra money for the big adventure we were planning.

We left from Cam's home in Homer, Michigan at 7:40 a.m. on August 28, 1968, but we did not take the most direct route to California. Neither of us had traveled much so we wanted to see a lot of sights along the way. In fact, we went way south to Kentucky first to take in Mammoth Cave National Park. We had no help with directions in those days from "Map Quest" or smart phones, or a GPS; we had to wholly depend on our skills of following a map. Most of the time I drove and Cam studied the maps. We traveled 445 miles that first day. The vehicle we were using for this trip was my 1964 Chevy Impala four door hardtop, and we had a good share of our life's belongings in it. We had to buy a car top carrier to fit it all in. The first night was spent in our tent near Mammoth Cave.

The next day, we took a couple of tours of the caves. No wonder it is called Mammoth Cave with its more than 400 miles of interlinking caves. I'm surprised I was willing to go into the caves as I have a phobia of bats! (I guess I did not realize this until probably about six years later when we had visits of these terrible rodents every once in a while in our older home!) We also took a boat ride down the Green River and saw a lot of wildlife. Then we drove on for only 50 miles and spent the night.

It was morning and we were on our way again with the sun shining so beautifully and everything seemed to be going so well, BUT THEN . . . we were driving through a large town and Cam was at the wheel. She was taking a turn driving to give me a little break. We came to a very busy intersection and Cam saw the light changing. She was indecisive whether to keep going or to stop, and decided at the last minute to stop. SLAM . . . went the brakes and then, surprise, the car top carrier came flying off the top of the car! It went over the hood and into the middle of a very busy intersection which was mighty embarrassing to say the least! Some nice men came and carried it off the road for us, as well as a few of the boxes that had gotten dispersed about here and there. They did this all quickly to get out of the way of cars impatiently waiting to get through the intersection. We had to unpack the car top carrier and boxes, and since the trunk was already packed very full, we filled up the whole back seat and floor area too. The bent and now useless carrier and empty boxes were left by a store on the corner. The owner of the store said he could dispose of it for us. That day we traveled 335 miles and had a hard time finding any camping areas in Illinois. We wound up staying in a cabin for only five dollars, which was a good thing after our troubling day with the car top carrier accident.

We made it to the mighty, beautiful Mississippi River and crossed over it into Iowa the next day. Nothing too eventful happened that day, and we decided since it was Saturday, we would spend the night in a motel. We stayed at an El Rancho in Iowa with a beautiful pool, and it was only eleven dollars for the two of us. It had been a great day of traveling, and we again drove 335 miles. On Sunday we found a church to attend and only traveled 295 miles that day. We camped at a very primitive park with only little holes for toilets as the park was in the process of being developed. We climbed into our nice, warm, humble tent and tried to get some shut-eye.

Next, a new day, and we spent all day heading for the Badlands. We finally arrived and drove all around through the Badlands . . . they do not look like much but have a certain beauty all of their own. Then we drove and drove looking for some place to stay, but there was nothing available. We finally ended up in a nearby city in a motel. We were getting moved into our room when all of a sudden I realized I had locked the car with the keys remaining in the car! I panicked, but then I remembered, "Good, Cam had the spare keys in her purse," which she did, but it was locked in the car with everything else! We walked across the street to a gas station to see if they could help us. After much work, a gas station attendant got the car unlocked using a hanger through the top of the window! We were so happy! It had been a long day as we drove 618 miles.

We were up early the next morning and went back to the Badlands to explore them more and get pictures. It was very interesting to see the different formations and to read how each one was formed. After enjoying the little chipmunks living in the Badlands, we went on to the Black Hills and Mt. Rushmore. The most exciting thing we did this day was take a helicopter ride over Mt. Rushmore. It was so much fun to look out and see everywhere! To see Mt. Rushmore up close like that was thrilling indeed! We also went to a dog race, since we just wanted to watch one once and see how it all was done (no betting for us though!). We stayed in a cheap little cabin that night since frost was predicted (242 miles of traveling that day).

Mt. Rushmore Cave was next on our agenda. It was okay, but we both liked Mammoth Cave much better. Then we really enjoyed our drive on Skyline Drive and the Red Carpet Tour where we could see for miles around---really a sight to behold! We visited a dinosaur park and headed back to our little cabin. The following day was a lot of driving (435 miles) as we headed to Yellowstone National Park. That night our stay was in Cody, which was 40 miles from Yellowstone. We saw the Buffalo Bill

Dam built from 1905 to 1910, and it is 328 feet high. The dam was made entirely with horses. The best team of horses lost their lives, because they fell into the cement when the dam was being built.

The next day we went through six tunnels in the mountains, dug right through the rock. We saw many sights in Yellowstone, which of course, included Old Faithful. Yellowstone, established in 1872, is the oldest National Park and contains about 3,400 square miles of Wyoming. Several of the mountains are over 11,000 feet high. We saw eight bears right along the road begging people to feed them, and we saw a couple of moose. We did a lot of riding around enjoying Yellowstone (160 miles), then Cam and I stayed in a motel near Mammoth Hot Springs.

Next, we drove on to the state of Washington. We called our folks that night to let them know how things were going. Our motel for the night was very nice in the big city of Coeur d'Alene, Idaho. 470 miles was our accomplishment for that day.

The following day we made it to my cousins' house in Seattle and drove over 600 miles that day. After spending the night with them, the next day the cousins drove us all around in the big city of Seattle. We went up the Space Needle which is 605 feet high, and it takes only 43 seconds to get to the top in the elevator. You can see the city out of the windows while riding in the elevator. We spent the night at my second-cousin Betty's apartment. The next day she took us to Mt. Rainier, a two hour drive, but well worth it as such a beautiful mountain! We went for a short hike there breathing in the fresh mountain air and taking in the beauty all around us. Mt. Rainier stands majestically at 14,410 feet above sea level and has 26 glaciers. During some of the biggest winters, as much as 50 to 60 feet of snow falls.

The next morning we traveled on to California. We spent the night in Canyonville, Oregon. Then another new day and a big day of traveling with a new record . . . 750 miles in one day! We made it almost to San Francisco before we stopped for the night. We left San Francisco for another long day on the road trying to get to Cam's uncle's place. Arriving in the Los Angeles area at 8:30 p.m. was not fun, trying to find our way in the dark on those huge freeways with all the fast-moving cars. This made me a bit scared driving in the big city at night, and seeing some rough-looking characters did not help matters any. When it got to be 9:30 p.m., we gave up driving and grabbed a motel in Pasadena, one of the nicest motels we stayed at on our whole trip and for a very reasonable price (513 miles that day).

In the morning we found out we were only ten miles from Cam's Uncle Leroy's place. So we could have easily made it there yet the previous night, but that would have been very late to drop in on someone. Our long anticipated trip and dream of going to California had come to an end, and we were rather disappointed as we loved traveling. We stayed at Cam's uncle and aunt's home from Saturday night through Tuesday night. They were so wonderful to us . . . friendly and very hospitable. They went out of their way to make us feel welcome and at home with them and their three children.

We had a discouraging day of job hunting on Monday, but Tuesday the Lord answered our prayers above and beyond what we could have imagined. We both acquired a job at the same small hospital, and then we found a furnished apartment kitty-corner across from the hospital. That same week on Wednesday Cam started to work, and I moved our belongings into our new home. The following Monday, I started to work. That just goes to show, we should be less anxious about our tomorrows and have more faith! Our adventure was from August 28 until September 14, and we traveled 5,365 miles.

Yes, it was quite an unusual and daring adventure for two young ladies to go all that way alone across the United States. It took us a long time to finally reach our destination because we stopped to see so many famous places along the way. I enjoy reading adventurous stories of pioneers heading west in their covered wagons. At least as we traveled across the states we did not have to face all of the obstacles of those brave pioneers like surmount impossible mountain passes, cross rushing and turbulent rivers, travel on and on in the burning hot deserts, worry about our food and water supply, or perhaps face a Native American war party. Plus, our two and a half week trip was very good when you realize wagon trains could only make sixteen miles some days!

We were so thankful to travel such a great distance with no car troubles, fender-benders, illness, flat tires or any problems (other than losing our car top carrier). God was with us and perhaps His *guardian* and *mighty angels* were protecting us with His watchcare each mile of the way. It was nice to have had a destination . . . Cam's uncle and aunt's house, and a place to stay while looking for work and an apartment. When people heard of our planned trip, many made comments and said, "You will never find a job in California." But look how quickly we found work and jobs that we liked. I worked in the surgery department. I transferred patients on gurneys from their room to the surgery department, cleaned and autoclaved the surgical instruments after the surgeries, and placed the instruments in packs in perfect order for the next surgeries. Cam worked in the cafeteria, and it was not very long before she became the manager of the cafeteria. We lived only two blocks from Cam's uncle and aunt and often did things with them or had a meal with them. They were our family away from home. We lived in California for close to two years and enjoyed living there very much! We took in all the sights we could while living there which included Disneyland many times. My folks and aunt came out to visit us while we were living there as well as Cam's folks, and a friend of mine and a friend of Cam's. We liked our very nice apartment with a pool and beautiful view, enjoyed our work, and there were so many interesting things to see and do.

After we lived there for a while, we decided we wanted to go and spend the day at the ocean, which was only about forty miles away. So we packed up our gear and headed west. We soon were having a wonderful time delighting in the ocean breezes, swimming, relaxing and enjoying the sound of the loud, crashing waves, watching people, reading, and watching seagulls (one of my favorite birds). We had packed a picnic lunch and stayed there until late afternoon. Later, when we were home we soon noticed that we had gotten sunburned and very badly! We had a restless, painful night of sleep. We had gone to the ocean on Saturday, and when I went to work on Monday my face, arms, and shoulders were still a bright red. I was like a red lobster! My boss, Sister Francis Xavier, felt sorry for me and got some cream which she applied on my face several times that day. We knew we were not true Californians since they know how badly you can burn at the ocean with the hot sun and the breeze off the water. We never made that mistake again. It was the worst sunburn I ever had in my life!

LITTLE ANGELS AND MIGHTY ANGELS

I mentioned when I wrote my first book, *A Farm Girl's Memories*, I never was one who kept journals. So I have to rely a lot on my memory. However, for our trip to California and back, we kept a trip diary. I usually kept trip diaries on our many trips after I was married. I emailed Cam and asked her to help out with some memories of our stay in California. She reminded me of our weekend excursion to check out Palm Springs, since we had always heard so much about it. It has a tram that goes from the desert up to the mountain top nearby. That looked enjoyable to us so we purchased our tickets and hopped on with the others. I was enjoying the view, and we were nearing the top when all of a sudden Cam said, "Judy, I don't feel so good!" I just told her "Never mind, we are almost to the top. Be quiet; you're okay." When they opened the door of the tram to let us out, Cam proceeded to fall out and fell on the floor. She had passed out! The people working up there had smelling salts, because many people pass out with the quick altitude change of 6000 feet in a ten-minute ride. We always laugh at that story, because I had told Cam to be quiet and then she just passed out. This tram first opened September 1963 and is the largest rotating aerial tramway in the world. It starts out in the desert at 2,643 feet and ends at the mountain top with an elevation of 8,516 feet. There are two restaurants at the top with breathtaking views of the valley below. The tram travels over two-and-one half miles, and it is 30 to 40 degrees cooler on top of the mountain than at the bottom in the desert.

Another memorable trip was when we went to see beautiful Yosemite National Park over an extended weekend. The terrible heat was one of the things that made it memorable. As we traveled through the deserts to get there, it was 114 degrees, and we had no air conditioning in the car! I was very concerned about my older car making it, since every so often we would see a car stopped alongside the road overheated. I watched the heat gauge carefully, and it did go up some, but was okay. We got thirsty too, riding in that terribly hot weather, and I do not believe we had water along to drink. I remember stopping at some place to get a glass of water, and they charged us one dollar which was pretty high in those days! A funny thing was I had my left arm out of the window, and Cam had her right arm out the window. We both wound up with one sunburned arm! Cam's friend Janet was along on this little trip. She made a big blunder and locked the car keys in the trunk at a gas station. Now what were we to do? A nice gas station attendant figured out how to remove the top of the back seat (thankfully, the car was not locked!). He was slender so he was able to reach in between the seat supports and felt around in the trunk amidst the suitcases and gear until he found the keys. Boy, were we happy about that, and we could again continue on our way!

We arrived in Yosemite and stayed in the Wawona Hotel there. Yosemite is located in California's Sierra Nevada Mountains. Some of its natural beauties are the giant and very old sequoia trees, the beautiful Bridal Veil Falls, and the granite cliffs including Half Dome. Some peaks rise over 13,000 feet. There are a lot of walking trails, campgrounds, and mountain streams. We spent some time crossing, wading, and swimming in one stream. It was very cold, but we had fun! We had on old tennis shoes as the bottom was very rocky. We took a two-hour horseback ride which made us sore. Yosemite is so beautiful with its waterfalls, towering mountains, deep valleys, grand meadows, and vast wilderness area within its 1,200 square miles. More than 200 trees are over 10 feet in diameter and more than 300 feet in height; they are so amazing! We did many scenic rides in the car, made numerous stops, and enjoyed God's beautiful creation immensely! Cam made the comment that all she could think of was that it must be a little like what Heaven will look like. She thought it was the most beautiful place that she had ever been to before or since.

Another little mountain excursion of ours was in some smaller mountains near our apartment. One day we decided to travel up them for an enjoyable thing to do. So, we hopped in the car and took off until we were high enough to find snow. Silly us . . . of course it was warm when we took off, but up there at the snow level it was a bit chilly. We have pictures of us walking around and throwing snowballs in short-sleeved shirts and in our tennis shoes! Another place we could go if we got homesick for snow was to travel up Mount Baldy, located in Los Angeles county. It was only 26 miles away, and we could often see its snow covered peak from our living room window. Mount Baldy is 10,066 feet high and in the San Gabriel mountain range. One time we went up the mountain and rode the ski lift for something fun to do. It turned out, though, we were rather scared being so high with our feet just dangling down from the lift chairs. In 2020, hundreds of cars were stranded on Mount Baldy when the first winter storm brought snow and ice. Road crews worked hard to make sure that no one was stranded for the night, but many were stuck for five hours or more.

We experienced excessive rain and a high wind storm while living in California. The night of this bad storm, the winds got up to 80 m.p.h. The next morning we looked around and saw a lot of debris lying around and some roof shingles. I always parked my car in the parking lot right next to our apartment building. California roofs often have a layer of tiny stones embedded in the roofing. Well, in those high winds a lot of the stones were ripped off, and many small pebbles did damage to the exterior of my car, the top and hood---just like getting pelted in a bad hail storm. Happily, my insurance covered it, and my car received a beautiful new paint job on the whole car!

Another unusual thing for us Michiganders is that California has day after day of sunny skies---no rain at all. Then they have "the rainy season," and rain it does!---straight for a couple weeks at least! Pretty soon you are walking in water in parking lots, driving in water on the streets, and with water flowing just everywhere. I remember one day when Cam walked home from work (kitty-corner across from our apartment), rather than getting her shoes soaking wet, she took off her shoes and walked home in her nylons.

Different people told us we should see Death Valley, so one day we took off to see this National Park. It was a four and a half hour drive and 270 miles from where we lived in Duarte, which is a suburb of Los Angeles. To list a few interesting things about Death Valley: it is 282 feet below sea level, so the lowest point in North America; it is located in Eastern California and is the lowest, driest, and hottest location in the United States. The average daytime temperature is nearly 120 degrees, though in the winter it can range from the mid-60s to low 70s. So winter is a good time to explore the park. 134 degrees was the highest recorded temperature in Death Valley in Furnace Creek in July of 1913. The valley is 140 miles long and narrow---only five to fifteen miles wide with steep mountain ranges on both sides. Not a lot of people live in Death Valley (as of 2020, it had a total population of 576).

We probably did not leave as early as we should have for Death Valley, and by the time we drove the length of it (140 miles), and stopped to see a few things, it was getting dark. We heard we should not travel in the valley at night with very few gas stations available, so we were getting rather nervous. We had planned to grab a motel but drove and drove only to find out that there was nowhere to stay. On we drove, getting more anxious and scared with no other cars to speak of on the road, and the mountains looming on either side of us, dark and formidable. Finally, we got out of the valley and decided to go back to our apartment, arriving very late after that four and a half hour drive back home. So, remembering Death Valley, we have some eerie memories.

We wanted to see all that we could while we lived in California, so we did a lot of sightseeing. Disneyland was only 30 miles away, and we went there many times. Other things were quite close too, like the Hollywood Wax Museum, Knotts Berry Farm, Busch Gardens, Universal Studios, Huntington Library Art Museum and Botanical Gardens, the famous Crystal Cathedral, and Long Beach with the Queen Mary. We went to see them all, and revisited many of them again when we had guests. Though the sights were not far away, you always had to plan around when the traffic maybe would be lighter. The expressways were five and six lanes going one way, so really 10 to 12 lanes, but you still could get in a traffic jam and barely move for a long, long time---and that never was fun! Other things we visited were Marineland of the Pacific, took a cruise on the ocean and saw some whales, visited Chinatown, drove by movie star homes, saw the Walk of Fame with actors' footprints in Hollywood, took in several TV shows like Truth or Consequences, attended the Rose Bowl parade in Pasadena (only ten miles away), went to the San Diego Zoo, drove up along the ocean to beautiful Santa Barbara, and watched the Rose Bowl football game when Ohio State was there. Also, we attended a very beautiful sunrise service at the Rose Bowl. We saw and heard George Beverly Shea sing at a concert which was a real treat (main singer at the Billy Graham Crusades). He sang until late in life and lived to be 104!

So, we certainly saw and did a lot while we were living in California. Looking back, what a daring adventure for two young ladies, but such a fun time and what a wonderful experience! God was with us guiding and protecting us while we were absent from family and loved ones back in Michigan. I do not think we would have enjoyed it as much if we were all alone and did not have Cam's relatives close by, and it helped to have a good church to attend (where Cam's uncle was the pastor). Plus, California is a very beautiful place to live with the ocean, palm trees, mountains, and sunny skies.

TRIP HOME, SURPRISE, NEW JOBS

"Show me the path where I should go, O Lord; point out the right road for me to walk" (Psalm 25:4 Liv. Bible).

After almost two years in Duarte, California, we made our decision to move back home to Michigan. It was a hard decision to make since we had such a nice furnished apartment with a pool and nice view, we enjoyed the warm weather year-round, we liked our jobs, there was so much to see and do where we lived, and we enjoyed Cam's uncle and aunt and family. But missing family back home and missing happenings in Michigan won out; we decided it was time to head home. I still had my 1964 Chevy, so once again it was packed with all our belongings. After spending the last night at Cam's uncle and aunt's, we were off on an exciting 12-day trip. It was very hard, though, saying good-bye to our California family; they had become close to us and meant a lot to Cam and me. We had spent so much time with them the last almost two years. But we must move on to meet new people, see new places, and trust God to lead and help us. The past two years had been enjoyable ones, and we had fun and saw lots of things. We loved our California home but also felt the pains of homesickness for our old homes and wonderful families. Now, as we again traveled down new roads and saw new sights, we prayed that all would be well and that our trip would again be a memorable one.

The following is copied from my 12-day trip diary about our return trip to Michigan:

5/12/1970---The first day was beautiful . . . sunny and bright! We saw so many abandoned shacks all through the desert. It is hard to imagine a person living in a small shack in the hot desert. Our first stop was Las Vegas, and it was just what we had expected it to be---one casino after another. This big city is lit up and active all night long. Since it would probably be our only visit to this gambling city, we had some nickels to try the slot machines. We did not win much, but we had fun trying it once in our lifetime.

We stopped at a Gulf gas station to fill up the car with gas, and it cost us $151.10 in all. They said we needed new tires and overload springs---and that is what I remembered Las Vegas for . . . that maybe the gas station took advantage of two young ladies. So we lost a lot of money there, but not from gambling. We stayed there in a motel that night which was small but nice. We went swimming in the pool for a while. We only traveled 295 miles the first day. We decided to have a motto each day, so for the first day it was, "With God everything is possible."

5/13/70---Our second day motto was, "Make the most of every opportunity you have for doing good" (Ephesians 5:16, Liv. Bible). We got as far as another Gulf station and had them check the oil and water. It cost us $27.27 since they told us we needed a new rear seal and transmission seal. Soon we would have a new car at this rate! After Las Vegas, it was 37 miles to the Hoover

Dam in Nevada for our next stop. It is one of the highest dams at 726 feet, and Lake Mead extends nearly 115 miles upstream.

Then on to the Grand Canyon today . . . what a sight to behold! It is so huge that I find it very difficult to describe. There is layer after layer of rock with different colors. The most beautiful sight is to see it at dusk as the sun goes below the canyon. Brilliant colors of pink shown over the canyon, and it looked like a huge rainbow. We traveled 315 miles.

5/14/70---A new day and on our way by 7:25 a.m. The motto for the day was, "And the Lord gave them a desire." We saw a few last views of the Grand Canyon and headed on to Zion National Park, Utah. What a beautiful place Zion was! There were huge rock formations . . . all resembling Biblical things. We went through a tunnel which was over one mile long. We saw five deer in the morning; they were so pretty. Zion is 230 square miles of spectacular sizes and shapes of multicolored rocks. This park has some of the most scenic canyon country in the United States. From Zion we went to Bryce Canyon, Utah. The rock formations there were caused by a very rapid waterfall. They were narrow, tall spiral-type formations---like a huge castle. Bryce Canyon includes in its almost 36,000 acres some of the most colorful rocks of the earth's crust shaped by erosion into a lot of fantastic forms.

We drove on through the Navajo reservation. It was really something to see the Native Americans dressed much the way I expected . . . in bright colors, women in long dresses, and men with long braids down their backs. They lived in little clay huts. The driving was very mountainous, but we did make 405 miles. We stayed in Panquitch, Utah for the night.

5/15/70---Another day and 59 degrees. Today we waded in the Great Salt Lake. It had beautiful scenery around it. We went to the famous Mormon Tabernacle also. We traveled a bit farther through the mountains and stayed in a small mountain village. Our motel was out of this world. It was the Stardust Inn in Heber, Utah. It was brand new and beautiful; the carpet was so thick you just sunk right into it. We had a colored TV, an extra long bed, a little round wooden table and chairs, and the whole works. The view from the glass front was of snow capped-mountains. We drove 335 miles.

5/16/70---The next day we started at 8:45 a.m. and our motto was, "Don't worry about anything; pray about everything." We traveled through the mountains again today. It seemed like we made little headway because of the hilly, winding roads. The main occupation through this part of the country is sheep. We saw huge herds with hundreds of sheep grazing along the sides of the road. We stopped travels early, and we enjoyed the beautiful heated pool at the motel in Steamboat Springs, Colorado (only 290 miles today).

5/17/70---"Griping brings discouragement; God delights in kind words" was the motto of the new day. We had the bad misfortune of being stopped by a policeman today for speeding, but thankfully I just received a warning or the fine could have been $300.00. We could not gripe about it after our motto for the day. After this experience, we got a nice start on our route but found out that we had gone 55 miles out of our way. We could not go through the mountains due to the snow, so we had to go around them. We put on 440 miles today going through Nebraska.

5/18/70---Hot and sunny on this new day and 90 degrees. Our motto was, "Become better acquainted with God." Today it seems as though we really traveled a long distance. At least, for once, we could look at the map and see our progress. We are through the mountains at last and can make better time, but I do enjoy the heights, beauty and majesty of the mountains. This was an interesting day to see how the farmers do strip farming. To me, Nebraska would be a farmers' dream land as far as flat land goes. The soil looked rich also . . . very black and moist. We traveled 416 miles, and stayed in Milton, Iowa at night.

5/19/70---Today was almost a repeat of yesterday except that we were in more hilly land. We saw field after field of young corn coming up. Another thing today was the numerous bodies of water we either crossed or went by. We went through the Twin Cities in Minnesota---which I did not enjoy due to driving in all of the city traffic. Our lodging was in Minnesota; we drove a total of 459 miles.

5/20/70---We woke up to a hot and sunny day and took off. Then after many hours on the road, "Oh, what is this I see ahead today . . . white birch trees . . . pines waving in the breeze . . . a most beautiful lake, Lake Superior . . . rolling hillsides with green, green grass waving gently in the mild breeze, the smell of clean air and fresh land . . . soil rich and freshly plowed . . . we are back in MICHIGAN!" After reaching "Michigan the Beautiful," we celebrated and went out for a delicious fish and chips dinner. We made 328 miles, and stayed in upper Michigan for the night.

5/21/70---After doing some shopping in Marquette, we traveled on. We were not in much of a hurry today. We experienced some lightning and thunder, the first time in a very long time, since California very rarely has a thunderstorm. Today we only traveled 267 miles.

5/22/70 ---We crossed the mighty Mackinac Bridge. It was rather disappointing with very gray skies, so we could not see much when we crossed. We went out for supper again at night and then spent a horrible night in our motel in Petoskey. It was a pretty place, and we could see Lake Michigan, but we had a severe thunderstorm. We had not experienced a thunderstorm like that for two years. It was quite a storm---and we were scared! More so because we realized that nobody knew where we were if something happened to us. The morning dawned again, though, and everything looked brighter. We only drove 71 miles today.

5/23/70---Last night we stayed in a crummy cabin in Ludington. It was dirty and cold. We had planned to spend two nights there, because we arrived in Michigan a little earlier than we expected. We were to stay in Ludington and drive the 30 miles from there to church on Sunday morning to surprise my folks. But one night in the bad cabin was all we could take, and we packed our gear once more. After we found a really nice motel in Whitehall, we went to Muskegon for the afternoon and did some shopping. By this time, we were beside ourselves with eagerness and excitement, since we were so close to my folks' house . . . should we just go there? No, for months we had planned to surprise my folks in front of church on Sunday so stuck with that plan. We even had Cam's aunt mail a couple of letters while we were en route so our parents would have no idea we were returning home.

5/24/1970---Well, we did it! We really surprised my folks in front of the church. We arrived there plenty early and sat in the car until we saw my folks drive up. Then we walked up and joined them on the sidewalk. My mom said she hardly heard a word of the sermon that morning. Everyone at church was also really surprised. Since Dad and Mom were not expecting company for dinner, my brother Don and wife invited us all over for a delicious Sunday dinner.

That is the way another wonderful trip ended. We were joyful because we were back in Michigan, but sad because our trip had once again ended. We were joyful because we were with family and relatives once again, but sad because of the family and friends we left behind. Yes, we were filled with mixed emotions, but very thankful for God's perfect and safe leading once again. We said we must not get anxious when thinking about finding work and a place to live, but we need to lean on Him and live one day at a time. We must always remember whatever we are doing or wherever we are "to be content."

Here are some interesting facts about our trip back home to Michigan. We stayed in 12 motels and the total cost was $134.58. That is hard to believe as it averages out to eleven dollars a night! We went a total of 3,850 miles and spent $86.44 for gas and oil. The total cost of food was $41.10. So the total cost of motels, gas, and food was $262.12 or $131.06 per person. (Remember our travels were back in 1970, so we could make the trip pretty cheaply.)

Our trip was over. We relaxed a couple of days and then reality hit, that we had to go job hunting again. We looked and looked . . . Muskegon, Battle Creek, and Grand Rapids. Finally, we both were hired at Amway in Ada, Michigan. We found a really nice apartment on the east side of Grand Rapids and close to Amway. Here the apartment we left in California was $125 per month, furnished, and with a pool; this one was unfurnished, no pool, and $175 a month. We gathered some odds and ends our folks let us use and got by with little furniture. It was a spacious apartment with two bedrooms, a large living room, and a deck where we could enjoy the view of the woods in the distance and a pretty white church sitting on a hill nestled in the trees. I often went home weekends and stayed with my folks and went to my home church. This ends this chapter of my life. I move on to exciting things in the next pages. You will have to read on to find why I call it exciting.

SNOWMOBILING, MARRIAGE, GOD'S GIFT

"For I am convinced that neither death nor life, neither angels nor demons, neither the present nor the future, nor any powers, neither height nor depth, nor anything else in all creation, will be able to separate us from the love of God that is in Christ Jesus our Lord" (Romans 8:38-39).

This chapter is special to me since it is about the events preceding our marriage. It is not the same old love story because it happened to me! On October 17, 2005, I wrote it down so I would not forget all those fond memories, so now I can refer to my notes. No more reading everyone else's love story for me; this one is the best and most special. It is mine and how it finally happened to me. Where did it all start and when? Well, it was a rather slow process but a thing that was so very right and sure; a thing that is becoming rare in this world of ours when marriage is not honored like it used to be.

I knew of this young man as far back as my high school days. I remember seeing him on only three minor occasions back then. A cousin of mine and I picked cherries with Dick for a few weeks one summer. I even picked Dick up in my father's old pickup truck, and we all rode together to a farm to pick cherries. Another time we were swimming in the neighborhood lake, and he also came swimming with his friends one evening. And one time, I took my cousins for a ride, and he came along. Anyway, just a few insignificant facts to point out that I knew of him, and the only thing that came across my mind at that time was that he was a likable guy. Summers he lived with his family about three miles down the road from my folks in the old home where his mom was born and raised. During the winters, they lived in Muskegon (30 miles away) where his dad worked and where they had a brand new home. Eventually they moved to the old house in the country permanently and did a lot of remodeling.

I graduated from high school and after living at home and working at odd jobs for a year, I went on to the Grand Rapids School of Bible and Music and graduated from there. The only other remembrances of Dick were summers and seeing him drive by to my cousins' place in his old '35 Plymouth. No more fleeting thoughts about Dick ever went through my mind. Perhaps, it was because I was almost two years older, and Dick hung around with younger cousins and friends.

Then, in the summer of 1968, our paths crossed again. I had worked two years in a hospital in Grand Rapids after college and was ready for a new adventure. This is when Cam and I started talking about our dream trip to California. First, we needed to save money for the trip. So after quitting my hospital job, the very next day I wound up working at a canning company ten miles from my parents' home. This was one of the local canning companies that processed fruits and vegetables for the area farmers. Cam stayed with us that summer and sold Avon for awhile before taking a job at the same canning company. Dick, after finishing college for the year, also came to work at the Oceana Canning Company as he had done previously. I recognized him, saw he was the same nice guy, and made a comment to my friend that there was a nice guy for her. The job I had running the closing machine (put the lids on the cans) left me with free time occasionally, and Dick's job gave him the opportunity to come by and talk with me every once in a while. I started looking forward to our little chats there by the closing machine. And one day at work it happened . . . he actually invited me for a date. He had his pilot's license, took up his boss's plane at different times, and wondered if I liked flying. That really appealed to me, as at that time, I loved to fly. So, it was decided we would go out for supper in class---fly to the Ludington Airport and eat at a restaurant right next to the airport.

I looked forward to this event the rest of the week. It was a little funny as during this summer I had also dated another guy a couple of times with the same first name. He also called me that week and I had a hard time deciding which Dick it was, but when I found out, I turned the other guy down. But alas, when that "well looked forward to" Saturday came, it was too windy to go flying. Dick, however, did not want to go back on his offer of taking me out for supper, so we drove instead. We ate out and drove around town a little, and he brought me back home quite early. That was about the end of any thoughts of romance, because it was the end of the summer, and Cam and I were going to pack and head for California. Dick stopped in a few days before we left, wished us well on our trip and told me to drop him a card if I thought of it. Well, I certainly did think of it, and wrote a few lines shortly after we were settled in California. We wrote back and forth a couple times and that was about it. It was nothing much . . . just a few lines back and forth from one friend to another over the period of a year. Then we flew back to Michigan for a three week vacation. I was hoping I would see Dick during that time, but he was not aware that I was home, so it did not happen. To keep the story moving, about all else I need to mention is while in California, I never forgot Dick. Then, after living there for almost two years, I moved back home to Michigan.

While working at Amway and living in Grand Rapids, I would often go home weekends to be with Mom and Dad. During this time, snowmobiling was starting to become the big thing (and even earlier). Dick had written to me in California telling me about snowmobiling, what fun it was, and that he had bought a machine. Well, when you are in California with all its sunshine, blue skies, ocean and beach, palm trees, warm weather . . . it is hard to imagine what snowmobiling is! Dick owned a snowmobile as well as my brother Don and wife, Arlene. Since I was often home weekends, Arlene said Dick and I should join them sometime on a Saturday night with their group to snowmobile. There could be as many as 30 machines going out for three to four hours on a Saturday night, then we went to someone's house afterwards for hot chocolate, refreshments, and visiting. So, I don't know exactly how it came about, but that was my second date with Dick after two years out in California--- snowmobiling, and out with Don and Arlene and their group. It did not take me long to become a real snowmobile enthusiast; it certainly was a lot of fun and enjoyable! We did not go on other dates at first, just Saturday nights and snowmobiling with the big group. We rode double on the smaller snowmobiles back then.

We were younger, and it did not seem to bother us at all to ride double. Many of the other couples also rode double---not many of the ladies even cared or dared to try driving. With such a long line of machines, the fumes were terrible when you rode towards the back! The group was forever having breakdowns. In fact, I don't think we would ever get through a Saturday night ride without someone breaking down. We would stand around in the cold visiting and waiting and waiting until several guys would figure out the problem, and maybe get it going again. Dick's snowmobile, though, never broke down.

As the time went on, Dick started asking me on other dates, and we continued to see more and more of each other. While I was living in Grand Rapids, we started writing letters back and forth even though we saw each other most weekends. This continued for the two and a half years until we were married. He had given me a special ring with the word "love" on it June 3, 1972 (sort of a pre-engagement ring). Dick gave me my diamond on December 2, 1972. To me, I always felt that God worked things out for us. Here I was gone almost two years and could have met someone in California; Dick could have easily met someone in college and begun a close relationship. So I believe God kept us both from getting into a serious relationship with someone else and, instead, brought the two of us together. I praise God for that and for our wonderful 49 years of marriage thus far. God answers prayers!

We were married in my home church in New Era on June 2, 1973. Dick's uncle, Rev. Howard Bolthouse, performed the ceremony. He and his wife were missionaries in Africa but were home on furlough. We had the reception in the basement of the church, which was quite crowded, but it worked. We just had the regular food fare that was more popular back then: coffee and punch, buns with ham, chips, cake, ice cream, mints, and nuts. I bought the food and had it all ready to go in the kitchen, and the ladies' group from church served it.

We had our honeymoon in Grand Haven, only about 40 miles away, at the Holiday Inn overlooking the water. It was very nice, and we went back there once just for remembrance sake. Dick could only have the weekend off as they were right in the middle of the busy cherry canning season. Later in August, we took a big trip to Mexico, but that was with his whole family. So, that is a lot of the story preceding our marriage (but not everything). Dick was fun to be with, he was a nice guy, he had the same values as me, we enjoyed each other's company, I respected him, I looked forward to being with him on weekends, and one magical night when snowmobiling, I realized I had fallen in love. This is my favorite love story because it is Dick's and mine! It is amazing how after 49 years of marriage our love only grows deeper and stronger! We hope and pray that God will give us many more healthy and wonderful years to love and enjoy one another. A favorite saying of mine from a card is, "To love someone and to be loved in return is one of God's greatest gifts!"

BUS DRIVING, WINTER MISHAPS, RETIRED

"I can do all things through Christ who strengtheneth me" (Philippians 4:13 KJV).

After being married for several months and pretty well settled in the house we were renting, I found out they needed bus drivers for the public school four miles from our home. Thinking it over, I knew that I could fit it in my schedule. With my previous experience of driving tractors and pulling long farm equipment, I decided to apply. Shelby Public Schools proceeded to send me to bus school, I became licensed, and I started subbing for the regular bus drivers when they needed a sub. Then in the fall of 1974, a permanent route opened up for me. The bus supervisor took me around prior to the first day of school to familiarize me with my new route, and I started my long career as a bus driver. The first day of school came and my morning route went well. However, that was not so for my afternoon route! Here I was driving along on my way back to the school after all the kids had been dropped off. There was a very steep, long hill by the Cherry Hill grocery store. Three-fourths of the way down, the brakes failed! I had already shifted down one gear and there was no time to shift down another gear . . . especially when at times it was hard to get the bus into second gear. I had just enough time to pull out the emergency brake which helped slow the bus down, but it did not come to a complete stop. By that time I was already at the main road (Highway 31) with cars going every which way, and the bus was still rolling! I had to swerve way to the left to miss one car, and a lady coming from the south had to swerve to miss me. Fortunately, I was able to make it to the center left turn lane where I was safe from the cars coming from the north. I maneuvered to the next corner and made it to the bus garage that was located in that block. What a thing to happen to me on my very first day of driving my new route! But I did not give up, and I had a different bus to drive the next day while mine was getting repaired!

That scary and frightening incident reminds me of God's constant care over each of His children. We should always be thankful for His protection and His guiding hand. Perhaps one of His *mighty angels* kept the cars from hitting the bus and from me crashing into a car! When I looked and saw all those cars, there was no way I could have made it through on my own. So, it is there as plain as can be; God got me through! He saved me and maybe someone else from being seriously hurt that day. Thanks and praise to Him for His continued overwhelming goodness! This is something we overlook constantly and do not think enough of . . . forgetting to praise Him every day for watching over each one of us!

I drove for Shelby Public Schools for a couple of years. My route took about 45 minutes. There were the usual challenges of behavior problems, especially from older boys who liked to make it more difficult for a lady bus driver. During those years of driving for Shelby, I did a lot of extra runs to sporting events, field trips, and even drove in a three bus convoy to Cedar Point in Ohio (about a six hour drive by bus) for an overnight senior class trip. I drove for Shelby until our girls came along and I became too busy raising our family. Later, when they were all in school and our youngest was in about 3rd grade, a bus driving position became available at New Era Christian School, the school my girls attended. After my husband and I discussed it, we thought I should apply since it was a way to provide some extra income to help with our desire to send the girls to private Christian schools. I was accepted, and it did not take long to become re-licensed for driving.

I remember some very rough days in those early years of driving for New Era Christian School. The kids were loud, unruly, and often walked around when the bus was moving. I felt that was unsafe for them, and it was a distraction to me for driving the bus safely and carefully. It took many years to get the children to know what behavior I expected from them while they were on the bus. My girls remember many times when I would return from my bus route disheartened and discouraged because of discipline problems. Plus, my route was very long and became longer each year that I drove (often one and a half hours). It was demanding to be alert, however, when driving such a long route, and it was harder for the children to behave when on the bus for so long. But, I stuck with it and drove for New Era Christian School for 23 years! Just like with any job, there were good days and bad days. As the years went on I became more experienced and the children better behaved; it was a good job for me. I was home when my children were home and had vacations when they had vacations.

One time in 1998 when I was waiting for a bus I needed to meet to transfer the high schoolers, I wrote the following; "Here are some of the reasons I should keep driving bus: 1. The extra money is always nice. 2. Volunteer time (the long routes) is okay to help with our obligations to Christian education. 3. It should make me feel like I am doing something productive for the school and family, a worthy job. 4. It gets me out in the world and I see things I would not see if I was cooped up in the house all day. 5. It gets me to mingle with people and keeps me involved with the school's activities. 6. I am a help to the school as I get the bus inspected each year and keep it maintained and clean."

I also enjoyed driving the bus when I could observe the change of seasons. I wrote the following in a devotional book I made:

> My bus driving job is joyous during the several weeks of the fall season when the trees are adorned in such colorful splendor. I just feel God's presence in the fall colors and marvel over and over what majestic beauty He bestows on His nature for our pleasure and enjoyment! I think also as we grow older we even come to appreciate this beauty much, much more! I do not see my bus kids looking out at the leaves and enjoying their brilliant colors like I do. Sometimes you look down a street and the sun is bringing the trees, yards, streets, sidewalks, and bushes all ablaze in dazzling yellow and gold colors. And for a brief minute I can catch a glimpse of Heaven and what its beauty and wonderment may be. How can anyone who has witnessed fall not believe in

a Creator God? It makes me go on to think of so many beautiful things God has created for our enjoyment: a beautiful sunrise or sunset, swans swimming gracefully on gleaming blue waters, a bird's morning song, a precious newborn's smile, the twinkle in a grandma's or grandpa's eyes, a rushing waterfall, the stars lighting up the darkest night, the mighty roar of thunder and the flashing of lightning, and the list could go on and on. All we can humbly say is, "Praise God our Creator and Redeemer."

Usually I did not even mind driving on the winter roads, because I felt pretty safe in the heavy bus that did not get stuck easily. However, I did have some close calls on icy roads. One morning our school did not cancel when most other area schools were closed because of the ice. The gravel roads were so slippery the bus would slip and slide. It also would start sliding while going down hills, and there was glare ice on some of the side roads. One time I almost landed in a ditch on a side road that I was using to turn around on. The bus just slowly, slowly slid towards the ditch. At another place, I had to go around a curve and then down a hill. Around the corner sat a wrecker in the left lane and two cars in the right lane. I tried slowing down to a stop, but again it was all ice with no way to stop. Thankfully, the driver of the wrecker saw what was happening and quickly got out of my way before I slid into him. Later, I had only a couple more stops when I slowed to a crawl to pick up two girls on a side road, and I found myself in a pickle. This road happened to be slightly mounded in the middle. I stopped okay, but then the bus just slowly slid off that middle ridge and onto the side of the road. I am glad the two girls waiting could stay out of the way. There we sat---I tried to move the bus, but it just spun and was not able to get any traction on the ice, forward or backward. I called the school, and parents came in cars and picked up the kids. One of the men dug sand out of the ditch for the back wheels and managed to get the bus out.

There were other close calls on bad roads during the winter. One stormy afternoon, I had just left the school with my load of passengers and was making my very first stop. I stopped like always to drop three children off and happened to see a car sliding towards the rear of the bus. I quickly pulled the bus up a ways so that it did not hit us. I let the two girls off and while their brother was slowly coming up from the back of the bus, a large delivery-type truck came zooming past on the right of the bus---through the ditch (it also could not stop with the snowy conditions). The brother could have been hit by that truck flying through the ditch on the right! After the grade school kids were all dropped off, I had to continue another 15 miles to Muskegon to pick up the high schoolers. On the way I came upon a car pile-up---two cars off in the ditch on the right, at least three in the ditch on the left, and a car way up in the woods. It all had just happened! The visibility with the snow conditions was terrible, and it was not a good day to be driving a bus!

I did a fair amount of country driving, so I always had to watch for deer crossing the roads. One morning I had only driven two miles on my route when I hit a four-point buck. There was no way to avoid it as all of a sudden it was right in front of the front bumper. It was still dark and it was rainy that morning making it more difficult to see clearly. There was no damage done to the bus, but the deer was killed. Later I found out someone picked it up and used it for meat. Another time a large deer came running full speed out of the woods and could not stop in time, crashing into the left front hood of the bus. That time there were some scrapes and a broken piece off the hood. I think the deer was okay.

One very close call happened one morning when picking up kids and it scared me to death. My heart was pounding rapidly for most of the route after this happened. Just as two young children boarded the bus, a car whizzed right by on the left . . . even though I had the bus's red lights on and the stop sign out. I think that car was going at least 45 m.p.h. It was 7:40 a.m. and was still dark out. Thirty seconds different and one of the little children, or both, could have been hit and very seriously injured when they were crossing the road to board the bus. I think God's *mighty angels* were watching out for those children that day!

Another very scary time was when I was driving away from dropping a girl off at her driveway. I was only going maybe 35 m.p.h., and was almost ready to cross the rail trail (for biking and snowmobiling) when a rider on a snowmobile came flying down the trail from the north. It looked like he was going 50 m.p.h. and was not going to stop at the stop sign for trail users. I was already starting to cross the rail trail at that point with the front of the bus. The snowmobiler slammed on his brakes and stopped just in time---making the snowmobile go crosswise across the trail as I finished crossing with the bus. I looked back in my side mirror and saw the driver tumbling halfway across the road. With that sudden stop, it threw him right off his machine and he went rolling. I was going to make sure he was okay when I returned on that road after dropping off three more kids, which only took a few minutes. But the guy was gone already, so he must have been all right. I am sure he will remember to stop when he is supposed to after that incident! If he would have hit the bus going that speed, I am afraid he would have been critically hurt! A very scary happening to be sure.

I drove a total of 25 years and did have a couple of minor accidents, but I was not at fault. Once, on my morning run (and four miles away from the school) while going through a very small town on the main road, a car pulled out just as I was going by his driveway. I could not swerve in the other lane as a car was coming from the north, nor did I have much time to react as the car was right there! Bang . . . it hit the passenger double door of the bus and glass came tinkling down all over the steps. The gentleman's excuse was, "I did not see the bus coming." How can you not see a big yellow bus?! The school had to be notified and some parents came to pick up all the children and bring them to school. Unfortunately, this was a newer bus that the school had just bought to replace the old bus. It had to be out of commission while they repaired the double door and steps. At least we still had the old bus that we could use for a week or two.

An additional mishap occurred after I had dropped off all of the school kids except for two, and was stopped at an intersection waiting to cross the road. A car was coming from the north with her blinkers on to turn left, and two cars were coming from the south. Before I knew what was happening there was a crunch and I was thinking, "Why is a car coming so close to the bus? She will never clear it!" The reason she was coming at that angle was she turned in front of the car coming from the south. I imagine that car was going 50 to 55 m.p.h., which he could do on that straight stretch. So, she was hit very hard on her right side by the other car, which resulted in her being pushed into the front left corner of my bus. There was another loud crash with glass falling all over---even way up on the hood of the bus by the windshield. By the sound of the crash, I was envisioning the whole grill, lights, mirrors, and bumper all smashed up by that impact. I remained in my seat and first called 911---it took four to six times as the phone did not seem to be working properly. They asked if anyone was hurt, so I asked out of my window, and they said the girl who caused the accident was all right . . . just very shaken.

After getting out and walking around, I was surprised to see that the bus was okay---just some spots of paint scraped off the very front of the hood. That was not the case for the young girl's car. It was all smashed in on the right side where the other car hit her, and equally as bashed in on the left side where she had been pushed into the bus. All the windows on her car were broken and shattered and the back two wheels were bent. I would say the girl was about a sophomore in high school. After the accident, a parent from school happened to come by and stopped. He was able to take the last two kids home. Anyway, I had nothing to do with the accident and was just sitting there waiting to cross---30 seconds difference and I could have been across the road and safe from the accident. Several people stopped to offer assistance. The police did not arrive until a whole hour after it happened, and I had to wait all that time as a witness. I went to bed that night seeing that car come sliding towards the bus all over again. It was not a fun situation, but it was a good thing no one was seriously hurt!

One of the most unusual things that happened while driving bus was when I took a load of kids to the Christian high school thirty miles away for a special chapel service. On the way home,

I was driving merrily along on the expressway in the right lane when I observed that a car was STOPPED ahead in the right lane. I quickly slowed down, and as I got closer, this car STARTED BACKING UP RIGHT ON THE EXPRESSWAY---in the right lane! I could quickly swing into the left lane and get by okay, but it was hard to believe that someone would do this! This person had missed the exit she or he wanted and so backed right up on the expressway to get to the exit (and not even on the shoulder!).

There is a "Bus Driver's Prayer" I like by an unknown author. "Please Lord, watch over me this day. Please help me remember to watch all seven mirrors, over two dozen windows, eight gauges, six warning lights, six dozen faces and three lanes of traffic, and to keep a third eye open for wobbling bicycles and day-dreaming pedestrians, especially teenagers wearing head-sets who are in another world. Please Lord, help me hear all train whistles, trucks and automobile horns, police sirens and the two-way radio. Please Lord, give me a hand for the gear lever. And Lord, please grant me the self-control to keep my hands away from Johnny's neck. And one more thing, dear Lord, please don't let Mary be sick all over the bus. And finally Lord, please watch over us all so that we can do it again tomorrow. Amen." Those thoughts are so true as a bus driver. I have often told people that I really liked driving the school bus, but I would enjoy it even more if there were no kids riding on it.

There seemed to be one or two kids each year that would have behavior problems. However, I did enjoy getting to know the kids from kindergarten on up---to watch them grow and mature. I had a lot of "bus kids" over those 25 years of driving. It was such a huge responsibility to keep all of those kids safe each morning and afternoon for 36 weeks of each year and an obligation I did not take lightly. I drove until 2013 so I was almost 70 years old when I retired. A daughter and her family had returned from Indonesia on furlough after three long years, and I wanted to spend as much time with them as I could before they returned to Indonesia for another term. Plus, I had driven all those years without anything serious happening, and I wanted to make sure it stayed that way. I did not want to ever see a child hit when getting on or off the bus. Even with all the warning lights on buses, it is such a burden to make sure each child gets safely into their driveway or to safely board the bus. Though buses are outfitted with the best warning signals, and car drivers are told over and over again what to do when a bus is stopped with their red lights on, bus drivers still have to always be on the alert for drivers not paying attention and not obeying the flashing red lights. We always have to watch for this to keep the children safe as they cross in front of the bus. Some buses are equipped with a metal arm that swings out to the left of the bus to make sure cars do not go past; I think that is a great idea.

 I let the principal know that the school year of 2013 would be my last year of driving. I just felt it was the right time. I liked driving and getting to know the children and their parents, but I wanted my days to be more free without always having those morning and afternoon bus run deadlines. The parents were great and usually very supportive, and I appreciated that so very much! They often sent notes or verbal encouragement. I liked driving my regular route, but I did not like the extra field trips. Nor did I like breakdowns when I had to drive a rickety, old bus from a neighboring school. After I retired, though, I would miss all the beautiful sunrises I witnessed on my morning runs. And when spring bursts forth with new life and beauty all around, I would miss viewing green yards, yellow forsythia, magnolias, pear trees blooming, service berries, and other trees adorned in white. Again, how can a person doubt there is a God, the Creator and Designer, behind all this beauty and wonderment? I would miss the changing leaves during fall time. And I would miss seeing rabbits, squirrels, deer, and other wildlife. During the winters I would miss the snow layered on trees, bushes, and fences making everything so picturesque. But I knew it was time to hand the bus keys over to a successor. During the 23 years at New Era Christian, I drove about 308,035 miles. With my calculations (since it is 24,901 miles around the earth), I could have driven around the whole world 12 and a third times. That is a lot of miles! So on June 6, 2013, my last day, I was thinking of all the "lasts." The last time to fuel up the bus, the last times for my morning and afternoon bus runs, the last time to go way out of my way to bring some kids home who lived so far out, the last time dealing with the younger, noisy kids in the afternoons, the last time to check the bus over in freezing weather, the last time to check under the hood, the last time dealing with breakdowns, and the last time walking over icy parking lots four times a day during the winters. I was so looking forward to being all done, so I knew that I had made the right decision at the right time!

 The New Era Christian School bus goes right past our house on the way up to the school. In fact, my own children did not ride the bus since they could walk to school or ride their bikes. If they were running late or it was a rainy day, they would put on our front porch light as a signal, and I would stop to give them a ride to school. They liked that arrangement a lot. The fall after I retired, I sat and watched as "my bus" drove by our house and I was not the driver! It was a very happy feeling as I watched it go by, and I felt almost giddy with the freedom that came with it. I never thought driving a bus stressed me out that much, but I guess at times it certainly did. The last couple of years of driving there were days that I did not feel quite up to par, and I did not feel like driving bus on those days. Yep, I made the right decision, and I was very ecstatic and jubilant about being retired. There were days I just felt uplifted and free as a bird! I like the portion of Scripture in Ecclesiastes 3:1 where it says "There is a time for everything, and a season for every activity under heaven." The end of verse 13 says, "and find satisfaction in all his toil---this is the gift of God." Also, in verse 22, "There is nothing better for a man than to enjoy his work, because that is his lot." Yes, I can say bus driving was a good job for me when also raising a family--- work that I could fit into a busy schedule. But the time had come for me to enter a different chapter in my life, and I was looking forward to it with happiness.

One last story from bus driving days that I had written down:

> I was on my bus run one day and this particular year I had to shuttle a couple little tykes to meet another bus to bring them to Muskegon. Today the little girl was chattering away as children will do, and then she said a few times, "There's no place like home; there's no place like home!" I do not know if she was thinking of *Wizard of Oz,* or thinking of something she had heard at school, or if she was just getting very tired of her long bus ride. In response to her statement, her little five year old brother pipes up and says, "There's no place like Heaven!" I

thought, wow, the perception of little children! If only we could see things sometimes through the eyes of little children instead of always making things so complicated! We are often so concerned over money and having more and better things, or whether our children will do well and chase a lucrative career, or maybe we are considering building a new house, or getting a more expensive and fancier car. There is no permanent value in worldly goods, however; it is all left behind when you die! Our thoughts should be gravitating heavenward and we too should be simply saying and thinking, "There's no place like Heaven." Maybe we need to examine our lifestyle. What are we pursuing? Does it have eternal value? Are we seeking things above or earthly things? Is it drawing us closer to God or keeping us from Him? We read in Colossians 3:2, "Set your affection on things above, not on things on the earth" (KJV). And there are many verses in the Bible about the brevity of time. Psalm 102:11 says, "My days are like the evening shadow; I wither away like grass." I think our focus needs to be heavenward like little Isaac said on the bus that day. Thank you for the great reminder, Isaac. Sometimes we adults need the perspective to see things through the eyes of a child!

STORM, MEXICO, PROTECTION

"Trust in the Lord with all your heart; and lean not unto your own understanding. In all your ways acknowledge Him, and He shall direct your paths" (Proverbs 3:5-6 KJV).

We did a lot of traveling in our married life---sometimes just the two of us, or with others, and later with our girls. The summer before we were married, Dick was involved in a Summer Training Session in missions (called STS). He went to Reformed Bible College in Grand Rapids for a semester after graduating from Ohio State thinking he had some interest in mission work. That is where he heard about "STS" and signed up for the ten week program in 1972. We were seriously dating then, so it was a very long ten weeks of being separated! This training program took place in Mexico where he made some new friends who ran a childrens' home, became close friends with a pastor and his family, and fell in love with Mexico and the people. Consequently we made numerous trips to Mexico over the years, since Dick enjoyed Mexico and visiting and encouraging new friends there. We went in August of 1973 with his whole family (his dad and mom, siblings, spouses, an aunt, and another young boy), and it took two vehicles to hold everyone. We always joked about taking the whole family along on our honeymoon on that trip, since we only had a short honeymoon after we were married on June 2, 1973.

Then in 1975 we took thirteen young people to Mexico. The pastor and wife from our church, Jake and Linda, who are good friends consented to go along. This came about because of our involvement at Newman Chapel, an outreach ministry of our church at that time. It still exists and is now an independent church. Dick was busy at Newman when we were first married...picking up kids for Sunday morning services, leading the singing for Sunday school, and teaching a Sunday school class. I also taught a Sunday school class for a few years. Dick became involved in Cadets (a boys' program), and drove to pick up kids for Cadets and Calvinettes (the girls' program). Next, we also became young people's leaders for many years and did a lot of things with them. We decided it would be neat for them to experience the culture of a different country, so we started making plans to take the young people to Mexico.

In order for this trip to become a reality, we all had to raise money to help with the expenses. The young people going to Mexico needed to help with this. We sold light bulbs in several towns, had a car wash, washed and waxed two small planes, and had a walkathon. The biggest money-making project was a huge garage sale (sold $835 worth of stuff). We used what we earned for food and gas. Our suburban was used for this trip as well as a station wagon that we bought at the local car dealer, and we sold it back to them after returning from the trip. We only stayed in a motel one night on the way to the orphanage, so there were not a lot of lodging expenses (In Mexico, the kids stayed at the children's home, and we chaperones stayed in a nearby motel). I kept a trip diary which I will include to explain about the trip. I think it was pretty unique to take that many young people all the way to Mexico. Many of these kids had never traveled before in their life!

This trip was a bit difficult for me as I had to leave our almost six-month-old baby behind with grandparents. Jake and Linda had to leave their little girl of about a year and a half behind also. Leaving little children is always the hardest on the moms, I believe. Thankfully, we were only to be gone for ten days. Now quoting directly from my trip diary:

> We met at Newman Chapel, and I could not believe that the day had finally arrived after planning and organizing it for so long. Several parents and others were there to send us on our way. The Chapel's minister read a Psalm and offered prayer. A few tears, many well wishes, and we were on our way at 2 p.m. on Christmas Day! Nothing too eventful happened until about nine or ten Christmas night. That was when we ran into one of the worst snowstorms in southern Illinois. It was snowing so hard that you could not see more than ten feet in front of the car. My husband drove through most of it, and then I took over, and they switched drivers in the other vehicle. The road signs were completely covered with snow and somehow we missed a turn and went eight miles in the opposite direction, sixteen miles out of our way by the time we discovered what had happened. There were also quite a few cars in ditches and stranded alongside the road. Once we thought we

lost the station wagon behind us, but we found out later that Pastor Jake had slowed way down after he had seen a car right in back of him spin around and slide off into the median. Dick mentioned that it would have been beautiful to see all that snow in the daylight! All together we lost about three hours in that blizzard. I think one of the girls was trying to see the bright side of things in all that stormy weather and told us to look at the big moon. She mistakenly took a Marathon gas station sign for the moon!

I do not know how long the storm lasted since I slept some. Everyone tried to get some sleep and would conk out in some weird positions. After driving through the night, we stopped in Arkansas at 7:30 a.m. for breakfast. We "normal" people ordered pancakes, toast, and eggs, but three of the boys ordered cheeseburgers and french fries with ketchup for breakfast. That did not sound good!

Then we were off again. It sure seemed good to see scenery again after that dark night. It was different from Michigan with land as flat as a stamp, with few trees, and a lot of cows. After lots of riding, we arrived at Texarkana, the border of Texas. The sun was out, rather hot, and not a bit of snow anywhere. Soon we were about 50 or 60 miles into Texas, and it became very hot. We were heading to Loredo, and our estimated time of arrival was 11:30 at night. Texas is a very long state and what long, straight roads!

It was so beautiful as we traveled past Austin when the sun was setting. The colors in the sky were fantastic---the Capitol building stood out strikingly against the red sky, a beautiful sight! And to see all the lights in the large cities at night was so pretty. We ate supper in San Antonio at a Jack in the Box. Finally, we arrived in Loredo at 11 p.m. on December 26th. Everyone was very tired and anxious to crawl into bed. That was a very long stretch due to losing three hours in the storm, plus longer stops for supper, and extra time at gas stations with our large group. God was guiding us all the way, and we were so thankful to arrive safely after all of that traveling. After a good night of sleep, except for some dogs barking, we had breakfast, prayer, and packed up. We drove to a Sanborns to exchange money.

Dick was relieved that the border crossing went well! No troubles with papers or the alfalfa seed that we had brought for the children's home administrator. They did not even open one suitcase! We enjoyed the sunshine, blue skies, 65-70 degree weather, and the beautiful mountain views. We traveled on and ate lunch at a Kentucky Fried Chicken in Saltillo at 2:30 p.m. A funny thing happened there with Ken. He ordered a different kind of pop in Spanish because he wanted to find out what kind it was. To his great surprise they came back with three cans of beer! When he said no, they came back again with a bottle of beer. Finally, he gave up and just sat down. We then had a five to six hour drive to San Luis Potosi [our destination]. We pulled into Sands (motel and restaurant) about 8:45 p.m. and had a delicious supper. We were all tired and grubby looking, but they gave us excellent service.

Next, we drove out to the children's home. It took awhile to get the kids bedded down there as it was already after 10 p.m. Then Pastor Jake, Linda, Dick and I went to our motel, and we did not get to sleep until close to 12:30 p.m. On Sunday we picked up our group for church and went to our pastor friend's small church. This is the church where Dick helped lay the foundation and put up blocks about eight tiers high when he served on

STS. Back to the orphanage for a dinner of beef, baked potatoes, beans, rice, pan (a delicious roll), and a banana drink. After dinner, the owners of the orphanage, Ted and Wanda Murray, took us downtown San Luis Potosi, and we walked around a bit looking over the town and sights and meandering through the market. We went into Templo del Carmen and saw all the beautiful gold work. It always amazed my husband and me that some of these churches were so magnificent with all their gold decorations while many people in the area were very poor. Back to the orphanage for some resting and visiting, and then to church at night where Ted and Wanda attend. That in itself was an experience since we all rode to church with Ted, standing in the back of his enclosed big truck. It was something . . . all of us in the back of that truck with no side windows, trying to keep our balance over the bumpiest road around . . . for sure, a different way to go to church! The service was in Spanish which we could not understand, but Ted gave a little summary when we got back to the children's home. The orphanage in 1975 had 49 children, one being a 14-month-old baby. They were kept plenty busy with all those children. The school age children had to be transported to school each day and picked up again in the afternoon. It was too far to walk or ride bikes and there was no bus service. There was another orphanage independent of Murrays' children's home but on their property. Two single girls were running this orphanage and taking care of 18 children all under the age of nine (and 12 or 13 of them were toddlers!). What a handful and what a lot of work the two young ladies had, and what a lot of diapers to change!

Monday, December 29, we were up very early. We drove over and picked up the kids at the orphanage, had hot chocolate and a roll, gassed up the vehicles, and were on the road with our large group shortly after 6:30 a.m. Our plans were to be in Mexico City by noon as we were expected there at lunch time. We stayed at the Wycliffe facilities in Mexico City and took it a little easier on Monday. We rode around some, and went to a modern supermarket to let the group see how the higher class people shop.

On Tuesday, we had our breakfast at Wycliffe and headed to the pyramids. They are located about 30 miles outside of Mexico City. There are two famous pyramids there called The Temple of the Sun, 216 feet high and one of the largest structures of this type in the western hemisphere, and The Temple of the Moon. It was quite a feat to climb the Sun pyramid, except no problem at all for the energetic young people. We were glad they made it up and down again safely as there were places where it was very steep and without railings. We older people did it too; Dick and I had been up it before. The kids talked a lot about their buying experiences at the pyramids. They got quite a kick out of it. This was the first time vendors followed them around trying to get them to buy trinkets, and bartered with them until the prices seemed pretty low.

After the pyramids, we headed back to Mexico City in smog so bad you could almost use the headlights. Last night the smog was not bad in the city, and we were able to witness the beautiful sight of the twin peaks which is a rare sight because of the fog. The locals call them El Popo and La Izta, and they are inactive volcanoes. We had lunch and then went to the National Museum of Anthropology, a very nice, modern museum and the one most visited in Mexico. We also stopped at the University to see a mural depicting the Olympics which were held in Mexico City in 1968. Many of the buildings there are covered with spectacular murals, making the campus very beautiful and drawing many visitors to see this great art work. One of the most noteworthy is the 10 story Central Library building with a very beautiful mosaic stone mural. As I was writing this, we had a new experience. Dick was driving and we got pulled over for speeding. Dick had not paid attention to what the speed limit was along there. Thankfully, he was a nice cop and just gave a warning. He was not looking for a fast buck like we were warned some policemen may do in Mexico.

We had supper and a nice time riding the buses and subways downtown. The Christmas lights were very pretty, and we enjoyed the view of the city at night by going to the top of the Latin American Skyscraper. It was a relief though to return to Wycliffe again without losing anyone in our group. We had given all of them the address of Wycliffe earlier in case someone got lost in the massive crowds, but they stuck together really well. I guess they realized the seriousness of getting lost in such a big city where no one could understand you if you asked for directions. The population in Mexico City in 1975 was 10,734,000! It is a terrible city to drive in, and we had two cars to keep track of and no cell phones. Then a nice thing . . . my husband bought me a dozen red roses which he could purchase for only 80 cents! And the end of another busy day. We thought the kids were tired and needed their rest, so we got back about 10:30 p.m. However, four of the boys still played basketball until 11:30 at night! [I checked Mexico City's population for 2021 and it is 21,918,936, so it has doubled in size, and we thought it was so terribly busy in 1975!]

Wednesday, and we were on our way again on a cool, crisp morning. In fact, most of us had our winter coats on, but it warmed up later. Dick had arranged with the person working for the Christian Reformed Church in Mexico City to give us a tour. He led us to his house in order to drop his car off and ride with us. His wife surprised us and served the whole group some lunch which was sure nice. First, the church worker took us through a cemetery that was as huge as anyone could imagine---miles long; it was so big! There was cemetery as far as you could see, and it must have been one of the main cemeteries for Mexico City. In the rich section they had little chapels and houses over the graves that were almost bigger than some of the huts that the poor people lived in.

We went on to see one of the Christian Reformed Church's mission churches. You would not believe the roads we went over to get there. The station wagon even got hung up on a rock! The kids got out and walked while a couple pushed it off. Linda even had to walk through the garbage that was all over the road. We handed out pencils and tracts---kids came running from all over. It is amazing to see their little faces light up when receiving just one little pencil! I think the young people all enjoyed handing them out and witnessing close up how the people live in the area.

The Christian Reformed worker also took us past the city dump with garbage as far as you could see; people shoveled the trash by hand too and not with trucks. It looked like some poor, poor people lived on what they could find in the dump as there were houses lined up alongside the dump. These shelters were made up of whatever was available such as cardboard and tin. What a lot of dirt, filth, garbage, and smog! We dropped the Christian Reformed volunteer off and went downtown again. I got sick and tired of riding in Mexico City with all the close calls, going through red lights with cars coming way too close and almost plowing into the side of our car. It was a relief to go to San Juan Market in the afternoon and walk for a change instead of taking all those chances in the traffic. Once we were caught in a huge, busy intersection as the traffic was plugged up and there was nowhere to go. The light turned green for the other people and here they all came at you---a couple sure did not look like they were going to stop! It was a wonder we did not see many more accidents the way they drive down there. It was always such a relief to get where you were going and back again safely!

Down at the market, everyone seemed happy with all they bought and bargained for. Next, another encounter with a policeman [on foot]. He motioned us over and Dick tried to figure out what we did wrong. We found out we did not do anything; he just wanted money. Pastor Jake mistakenly gave him his driver's license, so he had to pay eight dollars to get his license back. Next, to a supermarket for the group's breakfast in the morning. Linda and I enjoyed shopping by picture since everything was in Spanish. We spent our last night in Mexico City at Wycliffe. We ate supper, had a time of devotions and fellowship, listened to a Wycliffe man give his testimony, and then went to bed early for once. [Wycliffe in Mexico City was a training center for Bible translators who then went all over the world translating the Bible into the peoples' own languages. It was also a place where Bible translators could come for meetings and to recuperate, meet other workers, and take a little reprieve. It was a large facility with dormitories, a dining hall, a post office, and rooms for classes and meetings. We stayed there several times when we traveled to

Mexico. We did not have to pay for lodging and meals, but left a donation].

We had a wonderful devotional time on New Year's Eve. Jake read and explained a psalm, we sang several songs, and there were a couple testimonies. It was a very impressive time, and I hoped it was as much of a blessing to the kids as it was to me. Then Dick and I went over to Jake and Linda's room and celebrated Old Year's Night by eating peanuts and drinking apple juice. We visited until a little after 10 p.m. and then we left for our own room to get a good night's rest.

On Thursday morning, January 1st, 1976, Linda and I got up a little earlier and fixed juice, toast, and coffee cake for breakfast for our group, since the kitchen at Wycliffe was closed because of New Year's Day. When Dick started carrying suitcases to our suburban, he found a flat tire. It is a wonder all four tires were not flat with all the glass and junk we had been running over. After the tire was changed, we took off and arrived in San Luis Potosi around 1 p.m. While at the Sands restaurant, I went up to get Linda and myself some water, since we were not sure if it was bottled water at our table. You have to be careful of the water you drink in Mexico so that you do not become sick from it. Well, without thinking I just went up in the direction where I thought they had been getting the water, and I pulled the handle. I was not thinking well as we had been on the road for several hours, and I was a bit sleepy. At first glance, I thought the handle was pretty fancy for water. But I pulled it anyway, and boy was I surprised when out came foaming beer! Needless to say, I was very embarrassed, and the kids and the two Mexican waiters really had a good laugh.

Next, we went to the market for just a little while since a few kids had a couple of items they still wanted to purchase, and Jake wanted to take some pictures. Then we went back to our pastor friend's and gave them Christmas gifts that we had brought for them. Too bad we did not have a longer time to visit with them, but that is the way the whole trip went . . . not enough time. But it still gave everyone a good idea of what Mexico was like. We went back to the orphanage for a nice supper. We left the kids and arrived back at our motel before 9 p.m. We figured everyone could use a good night's sleep before our long trip home.

January 2nd (Friday) and we were rolling on the road by 8 a.m. So full steam ahead with probably 40 hours of traveling if we did not run into any complications. That would mean arriving home to New Era early on Sunday morning. We listened to Mexican music as we were riding along. The traffic was good. Dick had trouble keeping the speedometer around 60 m.p.h. since the cruise control was not working. He did not want to go much faster, because the trailer we pulled for luggage and sleeping bags had two really bald tires.

Next, we were on the 38 mile straight stretch--- straight as far as you could see. Linda kept track of our funds for the trip and added up what was left and figured we had just enough gas money to get back with maybe $15.00 to spare! Just think, a couple nights ago the kids were still playing basketball and football until 10:30 at night in their short-sleeved shirts. The following night we would need our winter coats again.

After a long ride, we arrived in Nuevo Laredo at 5:10 p.m., and we still had to cross the border. We had been caught in bumper to bumper traffic with both cars on empty. In fact, the station wagon ran out of gas at an intersection of all places! The guys pushed it out of the way and used the five-gallon spare gas can to put a little fuel in the car. I think we must have hit the border crossing at the busiest time of the day. While we were sitting in all the traffic, I was thinking how thankful we were to have Jake and Linda along. I know Dick and I, and I am sure the whole group, feel we had the best couple possible along. We so appreciated how they fit right in with the group, how they mingled so well and seemed to enjoy our company, and their great sense of humor was helpful along with good spirits under some taxing circumstances. Anyway, we felt such unity as a group and with Jake and Linda and would miss that fellowship after we returned home.

Traffic continued to be blocked up all over the place. We finally were able to fuel up and take care of things at a gas station. It was almost 7:00 p.m., so by the time we went through customs, we had lost two hours. Once we made it through all of that bumper to bumper traffic, the actual border crossing only took a few minutes. They did not check anything or even open one suitcase . . . they just asked a couple of questions and then we could go on. At the Mexican customs where they took our papers, they did not check anything either.

We drove and rode all night, getting what sleep we could. There was not a lot to write about through the long night on the road. We just drove and drove---we left Friday at 8:00 a.m. from the orphanage, traveled all day on Saturday and arrived at Jake and Linda's in New Era about 6 a.m. on Sunday, 46 hours of traveling! Everyone was so tired. We did not hit any snow until Benton Harbor, Michigan. Then it was snowing and blowing, but nothing like the Illinois storm on our trip down. Dick was stopped by the State Police when we were almost to Grand Haven. This time it was because the license plate light on the trailer was "too bright." The police did not issue a ticket, however, and we went on towards home.

These then are my concluding remarks about our trip. There were ups and downs on the trip, a few stops by policemen, and a flat tire, but the good times and God guiding us safely over so many miles certainly outweighed any of the low times. I hope the young people, Jake and Linda, and Dick and I will always look back on this trip and remember how wonderful it was and all we have to be thankful for. To see how little many of the people in Mexico have and how simply they live should impress on each one of us how rich we are---spiritually, physically, and materially. The people though on a whole seem happy; they know no other way. It opens your eyes to the great contrast comparing what we have to what we saw when we visited in Mexico. What a good way to experience a different culture, the language, the people, and their way of life. It was a beautiful and wonderful place to visit, and it also enriched you by broadening your thinking and making you more thankful for what God has given you in America.

We were happy how well the group behaved and conducted themselves. Dick had mentioned briefly beforehand that he did not want any discipline problems. Well, we certainly thanked the kids and were proud of them. We, as well as Pastor Jake and Linda, enjoyed being leaders on that trip. It was our prayer as we experienced unity with everyone, that the young people also had a deeper unity with God, and that He became more real to each one of them. The fun times were important to remember, but we hoped the trip in some way had made each one of them a better person. It was a long and quick trip, but the contacts with people and the experiences in a different country should continue to be with everyone. It was wonderful that we all had the privilege of making this ten day trip.

I would like to think that God sent His *mighty angels* with us on that Mexico trip during those many miles, guiding and protecting us every mile and every minute of the trip.

ICE STORM, NO POWER, DOWNED TREES

"The Lord will keep you from all harm---He will watch over your life; the Lord will watch over your coming and going both now and forevermore" (Psalm 121:7-8).

A huge ice storm happened in 1976 and it will be well remembered by many. Because of the fury of this storm, we experienced firsthand our grandparents' plight of not having electricity, telephones, or many of the comforts we have become so accustomed to. That winter had been full of odd weather patterns, with January holding records for consecutive days of snow. The snowbanks along the road were the highest in years! Then February came and the snow basically left. March came on a <u>Monday</u> and with it a steady rain which would have been abnormal in other years, but not this year, since we had already seen much rain in February. I was scheduled for minor surgery at the local hospital four miles away, and had made plans for our eight-month-old daughter to be cared for while I was gone.

<u>Tuesday</u> morning brought us the first vision of what was to occupy our minds for the next few days. The rain overnight had

turned to sleet as temperatures had dropped to 28 degrees. Ice was building up steadily on the trees and wires, but as of yet the pavements were only wet. Already there were some downed trees which was normal during some winter ice storms. By noon, one could see this was no normal storm. It was still raining hard and ice continued to build up on everything. By 4:30 p.m. most of our town was without electricity, but we were fortunate to still have it, along with the church across the road. I packed my belongings for my hospital stay, and we drove our daughter out to my folks where she was to spend the night. The roads were treacherous and many trees were down by then. My folks' power was still on, so we were happy about that! Next, my husband let me off at the hospital. He went home and had power until midnight when the lights flickered and went out, and stayed out.

When my husband woke up in the morning on <u>Wednesday</u>, the temperature in the house had dropped to 56 degrees. And what a sight outside! Our large maple tree had lost some huge branches, and they were blocking our drive. The ice was close to one inch thick on the ground and over everything else . . and it was still raining lightly. He called my parents, and they too were without power. They said they had our daughter in her snowsuit to try and keep her warm. Dick drove through the ice to get our baby and found them in the basement carrying her around in front of their old range that they had lit for some heat. He then took her to his folks' house where there was at least a fireplace and a camp stove for heat. But to get across the frozen fields to his folks' place, he had to borrow a snowmobile and bring her in on that. After our daughter was settled, he snowmobiled all around with the neighbor and observed all the trees that were down. Dick said you could shut the motors off and listen, and hear trees and large branches crashing down all around! What an eerie sound! It sounded like gunshots!

At noon, while on his lunch break, Dick came to visit me at the hospital which had been on auxiliary power the night before. I was looking forward to going home in the afternoon when he finished work. Dick borrowed the company's 4-wheel drive truck and brought me home. Our house, though, was only 46 degrees by then, so we decided the best thing to do was stay at his folks' house with the fireplace. That night we all sat around the fireplace, chatting, and playing games. By then, the telephones also were out from downed wires. We had fixed supper in the kitchen by candlelight. Then we ate it by candlelight in front of the blazing fireplace. We found out later that many people were getting together and staying at places with fireplaces, or in nearby motels. At Dick's folks, our baby and I slept in front of the fireplace and the others stayed in bedrooms under piles of blankets.

On <u>Thursday</u> Dick drove to New Era, and there still was no power at our house. He checked the freezer, and the ice cream had melted and dripped through all of the food. He wiped up the mess and took the remaining freezer food to a friend's freezer four miles away. The weather was getting better again, and we hoped things would soon be back to normal.

But alas, that was not to be! The second storm started as a heavy mist at first and then a light rain, but with the temperature at 30 degrees, it started freezing again. At noon it was raining very hard with lightning and thunder as well. By 4:00 p.m. trees were falling left and right and many roads were soon blocked. Birch trees at Dick's folks (trees 30-40 feet tall) were bent all the way down to the ground. Maples were losing huge branches and sassafras and Chinese elms were losing most of their limbs. One tree branch fell across Dick's dad's car and left its mark. We discovered later that sour cherries took the worst pounding with many Shelby area growers losing 25-50 percent of their trees. My husband said he would never forget the sound of those giants cracking one after another, due to the heavy loads they could not carry.

Another evening meal by candlelight, and my husband became restless and decided to go to the Shelby gym and take a shower. He had to walk across the field to the road, slipping and sliding on the two inches of ice. The rain continued to pour and the lightning flashed. The "river" in the field came to the top of his five-buckle boots. When he got to the truck, a tree blocked the road to the north so he had to go around a different way south. In some spots the road was almost impassable due to overladen branches hanging so low and almost across the roads. The lightning made it a beautiful sight though. With two inches of ice over everything, the blue-white lightning made the most brilliant scene my husband ever saw.

When Dick finally made it to Shelby, four miles away from our town and eight from his folks, it was all dark with no chance of a shower in the gym at the school. The drive home was treacherous, but Dick was really impressed by the power company's line crew working late at night in the driving rain and electrical storm. The walk back over the field to his folks' house was another drenching ordeal, just an unreal occurrence with lightning flashing and trees crashing as the wind picked up. At night the temperature went up to 50 degrees and every bit of the ice melted before the temperature went back down to 25 degrees the following morning. But the damage had been done. The tired trees looked like they had been bombed in the war or had gone through a tornado.

The power in our house had come back on during the night, so we moved home on Friday morning. After my minor surgery, it was so good to be in our own home again! It was Saturday before my folks and Dick's folks' power was restored, and Sunday for many others. We will never forget those days. Five inches of rain fell in that period of time, and it all froze where it hit. The cherry industry was served a severe blow, and many people had damage in their basements with all of the water. Yes, the ice storm of 1976 will always be remembered with all of its power outages, tree damage, lack of use of our modern conveniences, staying at the in-laws' cold house after my surgery, giving our little eight-month-old baby a bath on the ledge in front of the fireplace, eating what we could find on hand in the house, and having little to do those days. How elated we were when the power came back on, and we could enjoy our modern conveniences and luxuries once again!

Sharing the events of that storm reminds me of God's greatness---His unleashed power in the fury of a storm. Man has made the world easier with modern conveniences, but God still is in control! When the storm raged for days, many were without power and were quite helpless. Yet God is not only in the storm but in the beautiful sunsets, in the majestic mountains, in the tempestuous seas, in the babbling brooks, and if we invite Him in, He is in our hearts! My daughter said I should include some of my poems in this second book, so this one ties in with this chapter and how God is in control of all!

"DID IT JUST HAPPEN"

A twinkling star way up in the sky,
A newborn baby's welcoming cry,
    A bird's glad song in the morning bright,
    The wind's soft whisper during the night;
Did it just happen?
No! God did it . . . that is why.

A tree standing so straight and tall,
An ant or bee---no matter how small,
    A stream flowing calmly along its way,
    The dawning of a beautiful new day;
Did it just happen?
No! God made them all.

A flower petal so white and fair,
A wee little child's golden hair,
    A tiny puppy dog's wagging tail,
    The blade of grass so thin and frail.
Did it just happen?
No! God placed them there.

A father's knowing wink and nod,
A farmer's thick and fertile sod,
    A plane soaring through the skies,
    The twinkling look in grandma's eyes;
Did it just happen?
No! They came from God.

A sinful life but a change was done,
A Christian with many victories won,
    A man who was blind but now can see,
    The prayers answered from bended knee;
Did it just happen?
No! It was because of God's dear Son.
    (Summer of 1968)

NEW ERA, CHILD-REARING, ANGELS

"Children are a gift from God; they are His reward" (Psalm 127:3 Liv. Bible).

I need to interrupt my storytelling briefly and mention some background here. It is all in my first book, *A Farm Girl's Memories*, but perhaps not everyone has read it. I grew up on a small farm in Michigan, in Oceana County, along with four other siblings. There, we were taught at a young age how to work and do our share of tasks to contribute to the family's well-being. We often worked hard, but we had time for fun and enjoyed country living. We were taught good family values and always attended church, catechism, and Sunday School where we learned what it meant to be a Christian and how to grow in faith. I went on to college in Grand Rapids where I graduated, and afterwards worked for two years in Grand Rapids at St. Mary's Hospital. Then Cam (a girl I had met in college) and I went on the big trip to California, which I told about in detail in a previous chapter. When Dick and I married in 1973, we settled in New Era, Michigan, a small town which then had a population of less than 500. We rented a large, older two-story home for four years, and then we decided to buy it and have lived there ever since. It was a good home for raising our children with three bedrooms upstairs and one downstairs. The only drawback was one lonely bathroom, which could be a source of friction with four daughters. My husband and I both grew up in the country---five and a half miles from New Era for me, and Dick only three miles from town (and we both lived off of Arthur Road). So we liked the small town of New Era and enjoyed being able to drive to the countryside within a half mile in all directions from our home. The location was not bad either since we could shop in larger stores in the town of Muskegon only thirty miles away.

Back to my story---by March of 1977 we were expecting our second child and were very much looking forward to that. I remember having this thought . . . I loved our first little daughter so very dearly, could we love our number two child as much?! But yes, of course, God continues giving more love for each new baby as they come along. The love for a husband, and then for each child just keeps growing and growing! When our second daughter came along (just 20 months between the two), I felt I was plenty busy. It was a good busyness, though, as that was what I always dreamed of being---a wife and a mother. I was busy with two little tykes and Dick was busy also with meetings and various activities---way too busy! I remember someone saying when you are first married, you should allow yourselves time to get to know each other and enjoy one another, and not to take on added responsibilities for the first two years of your married life. Somehow that did not happen though with us; Dick was elected to the school board in September of 1973, three months after we were married! Soon after he also became involved in the consistory at church, picked up Newman Chapel kids (for Sunday services, Cadets, and Calvinettes), and did lots of things for fun with various chapel kids. Many times he was gone almost every night of the week, but he liked being on the go---he could not just sit home watching TV. It seemed a bit strange to me as a new wife (before children came), so I went to visit my siblings and folks a lot of evenings during those first years. But, yes, certainly a busy time early in our marriage. We often had couples over for a meal and a visit, or boys over for supper and to spend the night. Dick always faithfully kept a diary from his late teens on. He wrote this entry once, "I believe I actually had a night to stay home."

We did have some disagreements about him being gone so much until I changed my mind-set. That is who he was, and it was important to him to try and make a difference in others' lives (especially younger boys who may have had rough family lives). While Dick was busy serving on committees, I was busy at home with our little ones. My priority was raising our children to the best of my ability, and I was a stay-at-home mom to be able to do that. Dick was not quite as comfortable with the "baby stage" which I so loved. When the kids grew older, he was good at taking them to lots of fun things and on special outings. He still was on the go a lot, often taking the kids and me along. When they became teenagers, he was much better at talking with them and counseling them, helping them get through the difficult times. So together, we could work things out with our parenting. I think the most important thing was that we were united in our ways of training and disciplining the children. We supported one another wholly in this area which is so important as parents. Children can see through their parents if they are not united in this. But what a responsibility we have when raising the precious children God has given us! Proverbs 1:8 says, "Listen, my son, to your father's instruction and do not forsake your mother's teaching." Then in Ephesians 6:4 we read, "Fathers, do not exasperate your children; instead, bring them up in the training and instruction of the Lord."

Not long ago, someone asked us how can they raise ALL of their five young children to follow and love the Lord, and not have one or two go astray like you see happening sometimes in a Christian family (even though they were all brought up the same). We suggested that they continue doing what they were doing: bringing them to church twice on Sundays (if your church still has two services), having them get involved in the programs of the church, giving them a solid Christian education, making sure they have good Christian friends, and having a time of personal devotions with them around the supper table or at another time. This included the children taking turns praying out loud also. We suggested one more thing for them that we could have done more of. Parents need to always talk to their children openly, freely, and often about what God means to them personally--- like how they see Him working in their lives and in nature too. Make sure they see Christ-like examples in their parents. We also frequently would have missionaries or pastors over to expose them to missions and Christian service.

Christian schools with dedicated Christian teachers (or homeschooling) or mentors in the church all help children grow spiritually, and help equip them with good morals and values to prepare them for the rest of their lives. However, our schools and churches cannot do it solely. Parents have to enforce that training at home and be worthy examples. Every day we need to be training and instructing our children in the ways of the Lord! This is probably the most important calling we as parents have in our lives. If we want our children to trust Christ wholly and follow Him, if we want them to use good language and have the highest moral values, if we want them to be respectful, polite, kind, and care for others---we need to teach them verbally and by example, and not just be hopeful about it (we need to do something about it and work hard at it). I have heard that those first five years of a child's life is vital in their training. If we have not succeeded in those first five years, we may have already lost them. We only have a certain number of years that we are blessed with raising and instructing our children before they will be out on their own making their own choices. When they are under your roof, work hard and pray much about helping them learn to make correct choices and put their trust in the right person (the Lord Jesus) as they travel down life's way. Then always continue to pray for the Holy Spirit to work in their lives! Children are gifts from God. We need to support and be proud of them in whatever they feel led by God to do in their lives, no matter what we may prefer. It is hard to let them go, but we must put them in God's hands and rest in His promises.

    Always be honest with your children, take time to listen to them, and encourage them. I know we may often feel like failures as parents, but we just need to give them our best and allow God to bless our efforts. I like this wise quote, "A man's children and his garden both reflect the amount of weeding done during the growing season" (unknown).

While I am on the subject of children, I think it is time to take a moment to explain my title here, *Little Angels and Mighty Angels*. I wanted the title to be one to catch people's attention, and if you have read the book up until now, I guess I have had your attentiveness. Maybe by the picture on the cover of my book you can assume who the *little angels* are. What do many parents think of their cute, charming, beautiful, adorable, fetching, cunning little children? It is my observation that many parents think they are little angels who can do no wrong! Others see them more truthfully and that they are not so angelic. But do not ever say that to the parents of these marvelous children! So that is where *"Little Angels"* come in on my title. I admit Dick and I think everything of our own children and love them so dearly and unconditionally. There may be times when we too think of our children as *little angels*. It is hard to put into words the love of parents for their children, and that bond continues down through the years.

Now regarding the reference to *angels* in my title. In Revelation 5:11 we read about "angels numbering thousands upon thousands, and ten thousand times ten thousand." Matthew 18:10 says, "See that you do not look down on one of these little ones. For I tell you that THEIR *angels* in heaven always see the face of my Father in Heaven." So this verse indicates that children have *guardian angels* . . . might they be smaller than the *mighty angels*? And this is just a thought I am throwing out. We do not have any Bible verses saying there are smaller angels, though there are many verses in the Bible about the *guardian angels* and *the mighty angels*. Psalm 91:11, "For He will command His *angels* concerning you to guard you in all your ways." So it means that those who have faith in God will be under constant care of His *mighty angels* (or we all have a *guardian angel*). Revelation 10:1 specifically speaks of a *mighty angel*, "Then I saw another *mighty angel* coming down from Heaven. He was robed in a cloud, with a rainbow above his head; his face was like the sun, and his legs were like fiery pillars." What a beautiful and pleasing description of an *angel*! God may send an *angel* down to rescue His children from certain danger or perhaps death. Another verse about *mighty angels* is Psalm 103:20, "Bless the Lord, you *mighty angels* of His who carry out His orders, listening for each of His commands." (Liv. Bible). And in Psalm 34:7, "The *angel* of the Lord encamps around those who fear Him, and he delivers them." An *angel* rolled away the stone at Christ's tomb where Christ was buried. From in the Bible, we know that an *"angel's* appearance [countenance] was like lightning, and his clothes were white as snow" (Matthew 28:3). In fact, *angels* are mentioned in the Bible 273 times proving how important these ministering beings are. There are verses that say they are too numerous to count (Hebrews 12:22 and Matthew 26:53). And in Matthew 13:49-50 we read of a task the angels may not like to perform, "This is how it will be at the end of the age. The *angels* will come and separate the wicked from the righteous (godly) and throw them into the fiery furnace, where there will be weeping and gnashing of teeth." *Angels* may be very bright in appearance, or some may be invisible but you can still feel their presence. Other *angels* fly (Revelation 14:6*), angels* pay attention to what we do in life, and they rejoice when people make their decision to follow Jesus. Christ is head or the authority over angels. They have free will, emotions, and they carry out God's plans and purposes. I Corinthians 4:9 states, "We have been made a spectacle to the whole universe, to *angels* as well as to men." So not only does God watch over us, but also His *angels*.

The word angel means messenger of God or a heralder which describes another role of *angels*. A very important announcement from the *angels,* and one we are very familiar with, is in Luke 2:13-14 when the *angels* appeared to the shepherds in the fields at night, "And suddenly there was with the *angel* a multitude of the heavenly host praising God, and saying, Glory to God in the highest, and on earth peace, good will toward men" (KJV). There are many other stories in the Bible when an angel or several angels appeared to people to give them a message from God.

We will not have our answers to our many questions about angels until we get to Heaven. You can take the *"Little Angels"* in my captive title to mean whatever you would like. I just like my title and the focus on angels. What wonderful heavenly beings God created to care for us and our needs, and to guard us in all our ways. We should always be grateful that the *angels* are watching over us, and will bear us up in their hands so we do not "stumble or fall." (Psalm 91:11-12). I feel that we are not conscious enough about all the angels in this world, nor do we really stop and think about them very much! I believe in angels and I believe in incidents, happenings, experiences, and events that show that angels are actively involved in our world. Throughout my book there will be different stories illustrating that perhaps angels were at work in my life and in the lives of others. You will just have to read on to find out how and what happened.

LONG TRIP, SNOWCOACH, MEXICO STORIES

> "Let the heavens rejoice, let the earth be glad; let the sea resound, and all that is in it; let the fields be jubilant, and everything in them. Then all the trees of the forest will sing for joy" (Psalm 96:11-12).

Like I mentioned earlier, we were privileged and blessed to have many opportunities to travel over the years. I am just picking and choosing certain trips to include as certainly cannot include all of them. I do not know how my husband convinced me to do those lengthy trips when I had to leave my small children behind. That was ALWAYS so hard for me to do even though I had family to leave them with and knew they were well cared for. He knew such little children would be hard to travel with. He wanted to see things, and if I would not have gone with him, he probably would have found a couple of his aunts or someone else to join him. And I did like to travel and did not want to be left behind either. I guess I went along with his ideas being the shy, meek, submissive, reserved, and accommodating wife that I was (little humor here!). We made many trips back to Mexico, and the trip in January of 1978 was one of them. I had to leave my baby at Dick's folks, and I think my folks helped out part of the time also. Kristi would have been only ten months at the time, and it was so hard for me to leave her!

I am using the words right from my trip diary now:

> We left Kristi at 9 a.m. on a Friday and drove on to Chicago where our oldest would be staying with cousins (she was two and a half but excited about staying there). From Chicago we drove on until 12:30 a.m. when we pulled over to get some sleep in our Chevy suburban. Since it was in the middle of the winter, we heated our car nice and warm, put on snowmobile clothing, and crawled into our sleeping bags. But not so good . . . we were freezing after a couple hours [and why didn't we get a motel that night?]. By 3 a.m. I was so cold I could not stand it any longer! I decided to get up and start driving. Our intentions had been to sleep until maybe 6 a.m., so we arrived at my cousins' in North Dakota at 9 a.m. instead of noon as planned. It was just as well since the winds came up about noon that day, and the visibility was terrible. In fact, an uncle who had come down from Bismarck to see us wound up staying the night because of the bad driving conditions. The winds kept up their howling all night at the cousins, and we were wondering if we would even be able to leave the next day. The morning dawned with a beautiful, bright and clear day, so we decided to get started right after lunch before the winds started blowing again. We enjoyed our short stay at the Kuipers cousins, and Dick liked seeing their thousand-acre farm and learning more about it. It was 20 below the night we stayed there. We ran into some drifting snow on the roads as we drove into South Dakota. The drifts were mainly on one side and so with

not a lot of traffic, we could usually swing to the left to miss them. We drove through long stretches of desolate country, sameness, without much to see. That night we stayed in a really nice (but too expensive) Best Western in Gillette, Wyoming.

It was zero degrees when we left Gillette on Monday morning. I started out driving on good roads, but for the last half of my shift the roads were snow covered, and I could not see well when behind someone. When Dick drove the pavement was dry again, and it was very pretty out with the sun shining and the blue skies. We saw a lot of cattle grazing in the fields, deer a couple of times, and one time I am quite sure I saw a buffalo herd in the distance. Then there were larger "Big Horn" mountains to the left of us. We did not pass through them because they were slippery and had snow drifts on the roads. We did not want to put chains on our tires unless we really had to. We came into Casper and had a long way to go in order to arrive in Jackson by 6 p.m. to keep our reservations. Interesting . . . we drove through Natrona, Wyoming with a population of five! We just saw about 15 antelope.

We stopped at Riverton for a Kentucky Fried Chicken supper. Then the scenery was so beautiful! What a striking contrast! Beautiful plains with horses in front and snowcapped mountains in the background. I could ride in country like this for days. Dick too decided he would rather be a cow here than at my cousins' because of the warmth, beautiful scenery, and clear, cool mountain streams for drinking water. WOW . . . we saw such beautiful snow in the mountains---probably four or five feet deep at least. You just cannot imagine the beauty unless you witness it yourself! Dick saw the first moose, and we saw several more here and there as we drove along. Then right alongside the road, we saw a huge, beautiful elk with antlers. Next, we saw a few more antelope and then a huge herd of elk down in a valley. We arrived at our motel at 5 p.m. and stayed at the Wort Motel in Jackson, Wyoming. Dick did not have a good night of sleep as he was not feeling up to par. I did not fall asleep right away, because I heard a baby crying for about an hour and thought of Kristi back home at grandparents . . . wondering if maybe our little baby was doing the same thing, crying and crying without people knowing what she wanted like her mommy would. Then I had a twinge of homesickness for the girls and was thinking of how was I ever going to make it for two more weeks!

In the morning it was snowing quite hard, so we decided to take the bus to the Yellowstone National Park entrance rather than drive our suburban. Dick did not feel well yet either. Then we needed to take a snowcoach to where we would stay in Yellowstone at Old Faithful Inn. We did not care much for that mode of transportation---43 miles of riding in a closed-in vehicle with ten people, plus the driver, for almost three and a half hours! It would have been a nicer ride but there were such little windows, you could not see much. After a couple hours, we were pretty tired of riding in it. We did make some stops with pretty views, but it just was too long of a ride. Other than on snowmobiles, this was the only way to get through an area that could have as much as 200 to 400 inches of snow in higher areas. In the afternoon, we walked around the geysers for about an hour and saw Old Faithful erupt twice. The very best thing for me in the evening was our call home. Everything was okay and that was such a relief for me---both kids were adapting all right.

The next day we attempted skiing near some geysers. I say attempted because it was too much work. Since the snow conditions were warm near the geysers, the snow would stick to our skis which made it too difficult to continue. We left at 2:30 p.m. on the boring snowcoach once more. We decided we would never do that again. By now I'm sure they have better methods of transporting people in. [I just looked this up on my tablet, and the snowcoaches look more modern with nice big windows to see the beautiful views. It might not be so bad to try it again after all.]

We arrived back at our motel in Jackson and really slept well that night . . . best night of sleep since we left Michigan. I might mention that the town of Jackson, the largest town in Teton County, is located in the Jackson Hole Valley which is a 50 mile long valley. [We have gone through this area several times in our travels. On one trip our family braved the Snake River and went whitewater rafting and had a very scary and thrilling experience indeed! Dick did not like it and slid down on the floor in the middle of the raft where he felt safer. This is a very beautiful area and just writing about it makes me want to visit there again.] The beautiful Grand Tetons are only 20 miles away from Jackson.

Now we are on our way to Denver with a big day of travels again today. When I was driving through the pass out of Jackson Hole, the roads were snow-covered and slippery, but we still made pretty good time. There were about ten miles of real bad driving with mist and everything so white that you could not even distinguish the sides of the road. Thankfully, we drove back out of it and are on dry roads again. So it looks like we will not have to use our chains that we brought along just in case they would be needed on the tires.

As we are driving along this flat plateau in Wyoming, we keep seeing all kinds of deer. Now we just passed two huge herds of them, 50 to 75 in each herd. The last hour has been real pretty riding along and such a change in scenery again. No snow except in the mountains in the distance, long flowing golden plains, groups of horses grazing in the foreground, next a rocky, hilly area, and then lots of very pretty trees.

Exactly a week ago today at 9 a.m. we were leaving little Kristi at Dick's folks. We have seen and done a lot this week. Our stay tonight was in Pueblo, Colorado, and it was in the nicest motel with the best bed we have had so far on the whole trip. We had Kentucky Fried Chicken for lunch in Las Vegas, New Mexico. We are heading to Albuquerque today and will be picking up Dick's sister, Norma, and husband, Ben, and Aunt Rica at the airport tomorrow at 1:30 p.m. They will be joining us for part of the trip. We rode on the 2.7 mile tram today---it had two cars that were capable of carrying 50 passengers each. It took 15 minutes to reach the top with a view that was fantastic! You could see all of Albuquerque and it overlooked 11,000 square miles of New Mexico's countryside. I have been on trams of this sort a couple times in California, but this was a first time for Dick. There is skiing on the other side of this mountain in the winter.

We splurged and had a big steak supper at the end of another day. The next day we had problems when we arrived at the airport to pick up Ben, Norma, and Aunt Rica [she was called Re]. When we walked up to the ticket booth, the flight they were to come in on was marked "see agent." We found out the plane was down in Dayton, Ohio because of bad weather. They said it probably would still come in, but it would be six hours late. We did a lot of waiting around, went to McDonald's for supper, and back to the airport with more waiting. It finally came in---seven hours late! We still had to drive to El Paso, which was two hundred some miles, so we did not get to our motel until a little after 2:00 a.m. At least we could sleep in until 8:30 a.m. On Sunday we took our time getting ready, had a later breakfast at 10 a.m., and were on our way. For our lunch we made do with some canned goods and snacks that I had in our suburban. We had a nice afternoon of traveling and arrived at Chihuahua in northern Mexico about 6:30 p.m., found a nice motel, had supper, and turned in for the evening.

Nothing really interesting to mention today, just a long day of travels. The following day, we were ready at 8 a.m. for our approximately six hour drive. While yesterday's riding was hot and very dusty, today was a nice change---cool up in the mountains, crystal clear air, roads in places cut through some huge passes of rock, so very beautiful! We stopped at 12:30 p.m. for lunch at a pretty little hotel in the mountains. We bought our cokes and some Mexican bread [called pan] to go with what we had in the car. They let us eat our lunch at one of their tables outside. We really enjoyed our lunch in the nice little setting. The scenery on that route was so breathtaking, but you became a little tired of the many, many curves after riding that way for hours.

We arrived in Mazatlan, Mexico at 2:30 p.m. and found a nice, inexpensive motel. It was not long before we had on our swimsuits and were in the ocean for a swim. The water was perfect . . . a little cool at first, but once you were in it for a while, it was really nice. Dick said it was probably just as warm as Lake Michigan ever gets. We went to a famous restaurant called the

Shrimp Bucket for our fish. We went back to our motel, enjoyed watching and listening to the waves for a little bit, and went to bed early. I mentioned to Dick once, though I greatly missed our kids when on a trip like this, it is nice to think that my hardest work is taking a shower and brushing my teeth. The next day we had a really nice bus tour for two and a half hours around the town. We stopped at several little places with lots of shops, a place where a diver did a very high dive for us, and saw other points of interest as well. The rest of the afternoon was spent on the beach. Later we took a bus downtown to the market and looked around for a couple of hours. That was mainly it for that day. It is so pretty in Mazatlan! The ocean is warm and beaches clean with nice sand, or you can go swimming in the motel's pool. The climate is so perfect, and it is very inexpensive to vacation here. For instance, the motel in Mazatlan was $18.50 for five people with two double beds and one single which averaged less than four dollars per person. Norma said rooms comparable to that in Florida would cost 40 to 50 dollars per night without the motel even being on the beach.

Our next destination is the small town of San Blas, not a big resort town like Mazatlan. It should be real nice and peaceful there tonight, as we will be off the beaten path. The motel in Mazatlan was right on a very busy road. We found a motel in San Blas and booked a room which was huge and not too bad. Our meals were included with the room, so we soon headed out to try their chicken supper. The one thing about our motel room was we had to share it---with a little chameleon lizard. We ladies did not want to go to sleep knowing it was in there. It had crawled behind the dresser. Ben tried and tried to get it out, but it was hiding. So to please us, the guys carried the dresser clear across the huge room and brought it outside. Ben proceeded to take the drawers out one by one and finally found the lizard. We still were a little leery of lizards crawling over us as we retired for the night. In the morning we woke up to the roosters crowing. That little town was really different---one gas station, mostly little huts for houses, no restaurants or stores---just a market.

And speaking of little huts, many of the needy people in Mexico live in small constructed houses about the size of our living room. Somehow, they make do and probably know no other way. If they saw what kind of homes we live in, they would think we were extremely rich to live in such big homes. You always appreciate what you have so much more when you return home from Mexico. The time there gives you a new outlook on life. So far the vacation has not been too bad, even though I miss our girls immensely! No way could you take them along on a trip like we are taking. I am sure they are much happier and healthier right where they are.

We left San Blas and were on the road again with another big day of traveling ahead of us. Right now we are making very slow time as two big trucks are ahead of us. That does not bother the Mexicans, and they pass even if they cannot see if anything is coming around a corner. Unbelievable the risks they take! So we drove on and on, even after it grew dark, which is not advisable to do in Mexico. We pulled into Queretaro close to 8:00 p.m. I think it seemed like the hardest and longest part of the whole trip due to the roads being so terribly bumpy in places and so hard to pass. The motel we found for the night was fantastic! A little old, but it was still beautiful and reasonably priced. [In the '70s, the motels and restaurants were so inexpensive and were why we liked to vacation in Mexico].

Next day, our group traveled on to Mexico City. We are heading to the Wycliffe complex again to stay and rest from our travels for a couple of days. Ben and Norma will be flying back home tomorrow at 11 a.m. Re is staying with us. But first Ben and I had a daring ride on a roller coaster. It is boasted as the largest wooden roller coaster in the world! Ben and I were the only ones from our group who dared to go on it. It really was a thrilling ride, lifting you right out of your seat several times, and leaving you feeling a little funny when you got off.

We found we could not stay at Wycliffe this time, so we grabbed a motel. Dick met Ken, who was in Mexico at the time, [a former Newman Chapel young person who went on the prior trip to Mexico], and visited with him. The rest of us went to San Juan Market. It was quite an accomplishment for the rest of us to go all the way there by ourselves without Dick as our interpreter. To ride buses, change subways, and find our way back again was great---Ben did a good job and is really good at directions.

Today Ben and Norma caught their flight home and Aunt Re, Dick, and I caught a flight to Tlacolula, Oaxaca in southwestern Mexico. There we met Nick and Gloria, Christian Reformed Church missionaries, and spent time with them seeing their work down there. We visited a unique old cemetery with mammoth ancient trees. Then we rode out to one of the villages and visited with a lady in her little brick house. We stopped to see an orchard and the projects the agriculturalists were trying. The next day, we visited a couple more families in a few more villages. The first stop was very interesting as we watched a pottery maker at work. He did beautiful work using basic and elementary tools and methods. At another home, the man's livelihood was raising, butchering, and selling chickens and making bread. When seeing the families up close like this, it was sad to see the state of the young children. They had no toys or things of interest to occupy their time. The families do not even have a soft chair in the whole house to relax and be comfortable in. Many have no beds and must just lie on mats on the hard sand or cement floors. Most have only a small table, and no counters or cupboards. Everyone should see the way these people live to appreciate the great wealth and luxuries we enjoy in the States. Wages were so low in Mexico. Gloria had a maid come in twice a week for 25 cents an hour which was a good wage to many. And I am sure these families depended desperately on those little wages to survive. We also noticed how the service in all restaurants is unbelievable! All were male waiters, and they were attentive, aiming to please. We always experienced such good service, and the meals were so inexpensive! Oh, a frightening thing happened when we were staying with Nick and Gloria. It was common in Mexico to have the water heaters outside of the home as they felt it safer that way. One night we needed to take showers, and Gloria went out to relight the pilot light on the water heater that sometimes went out. When she came in she looked a sight! When she lit it, there was a small explosion. Poor Gloria . . . her eyebrows were singed off and some of her hair along her face and above her forehead was singed and black! After spending several days seeing Nick and Gloria's ministry, we flew back to Mexico City.

From Mexico City it was back to San Luis Potosi. It was the 26th today, so 20 days ago we left Michigan. That seemed like a very long time ago, but we have seen a lot in those 20 days. We again spent some time at the orphanage and then booked motel rooms at the Sands Motel and had our supper there. Next we went to our pastor friend, Jose's house. We invited Jose and his family back with us to the orphanage to show slides that we had brought along. The kids always enjoy watching the slides because many were pictures of them taken on previous visits. The next day was mostly spent at the orphanage visiting, taking walks, reading, riding to town, and visiting some more. Late in the afternoon we went back to Jose's house, gave their three young children some gifts, and visited the best we could with only Dick knowing Spanish. Then we took their whole family to the restaurant at the Sands Motel for supper. It probably was one of the few times they had been out to eat. Mrs. Munoz brought home all the leftovers, and I think that is what they lived on for days. Even for them to ride in a vehicle was quite a treat. Dick let the two boys steer the van on their bumpy dirt road, which was so much fun for them. It was special on the way back as the whole family was singing. They are such a nice Christian family, and they are always so happy to see us. Mrs. Munoz cried again when we left. We all held hands for prayer; each one of the family took a turn and prayed. They gave us some beautiful pottery the night before, which we felt bad about taking, since we knew it was a costly gift for them. We returned to the Sands Motel for one more night of sleep before the trip home to Michigan!

We are on our way north with more mountainous driving. This driving is always risky with hardly any guard rails in some treacherous places. One time we witnessed an accident in front of us in these mountains. Another time Ted, the children's home administrator, was riding back with us to the border. We rounded a corner and found a police car parked by the side of the road. Ted asked what had happened, and he said a semi-truck had just gone over the side of the mountain---a terrible accident! That reminds me of the cow accident we witnessed. We saw a car a short way in front of us hit a cow that was in the road, and the cow flew about six feet into the air---clear from the left side of the road and landing back on the right side of the road. I am glad we were back far enough so we did not hit it too! Another car had to completely stop or he surely would have hit the cow also. The car that hit it was passing the other car and must not have seen the cow starting to cross the road.

About 1 p.m. we had another lunch out of our canned goods supply in the back of the suburban. That really works out well for lunches, since we had to be careful about eating in little restaurants off the beaten path. It was wise to eat in places frequented by tourists where they served you bottled water, and maybe washed the lettuce better---but we still stayed away from salads to avoid becoming ill. Usually we survived okay when traveling in Mexico, but I did get sick a couple times from the food, and it was not fun! So, for our travels I would stock up on spam, tuna fish, canned chicken, crackers, cookies, applesauce, and pudding. Then all we had to do was buy a pop and some bread, or their delicious "pan", make some sandwiches, and we were all set. It was much safer healthwise that way! We called them our tailgate picnics. We continued on to the border, and this evening we should be back in the good ol' U.S.A.! After traveling so long in Mexico, I was always eager for a good hamburger, fries, and a chocolate shake at McDonalds!

The border crossing went well but slowly. They took both of Aunt Re's suitcases and one of mine, opened them and searched through them, looked in the back of the vehicle, and that was it. Then it was good to be home again in the U.S. Right after crossing the border, the countryside and alongside the roads look cleaner, roads are so much better, and the farmland looks so rich and productive. Oh, and I see a Rest Area which you never find in Mexico. Different thoughts go through my mind about enjoying our wonderful country in which we live. If Jose and his family could see it and all of our luxuries, they just would not be able to believe it. We so often take these blessings for granted! Yet to see the Munozes happy and see their closeness as a family is special, as well as their belief in Christ. They were so sad to see us leave, but Jose said Christ is coming soon, and then we will all be together to have fellowship with each other. Like we have said before, you come away a better person because of the things you witness in Mexico. If our Michigan friends could visit Mexico and see how people like the Munozes live, their lives would be enriched and their eyes opened to all that we have living in the U.S.A.

Another day, and we have been on the road for about 27 hours already. We plan on staying in a motel tonight, so it should only be a six hour drive home. However, we have been listening to forecasts of snow on the radio . . . we first ran into some snow in Texarkana, Arkansas and quite a bit more snow halfway to Little Rock, Arkansas. Then, troubles at 6 p.m.---we are stranded down in Marion, Illinois [bottom corner of the state]. We knew there was bad weather, but we certainly did not expect it this bad with roads closed! They are saying maybe for a couple of days! It is being reported as the worst storm in history with all roads blocked to the north. We were fortunate to be able to find a motel room. As a result of the storm, motels were filling up with stranded people who could not get any farther. Dick called the State Police, and I guess we can get through in the morning on 55 through St. Louis, Missouri. That will be quite a bit out of the way, but it is better than staying here a couple days. Dick called his folks, and they said everything was closed around there too and no one was getting anywhere. Oh, dear; when will I ever see our little girls again?!

Up at 4 a.m., and we are once again on the road. We had to go back west about 42 miles and catch 55 through Illinois since 57 was still closed. It was about 80 miles out of our way, but we were traveling and making progress. We had lunch in Chicago, and Dick talked to someone there who told us to take Highway 20 to Michigan City to bypass 94 where it was closed. That worked, and now we are as far as Holland, Michigan. We stopped in Holland for gas, and the station was out of fuel. He said many of the gas stations were out as a result of their truck suppliers not being able to get in. We will have to try again in Muskegon 30 miles from home!

We took back roads and arrived home around 7 p.m. on January 28th. No one ever saw a storm like this one. There was snow right up to the kitchen window which is four and a half feet high! We could not get out to pick up the girls as roads were all still closed---they were so close, five miles away, and I still could not see my babies. The next day was Sunday, so we went to our morning church service. Then a friend of Dick's snowmobiled into town to get Dick, and brought him out to his folks where our snowmobiles were kept. Dick could snowmobile back and get me, back to Dick's folks, and I could FINALLY SEE the girls! Kristi, at 10 months, did not even recognize me, and I really felt bad about that. I was concerned she would be walking while we were gone, and I would not be able to witness her first steps. Thankfully, she waited to walk on her own until after we got back from that long trip. After some visiting, we had to snowmobile both of the girls back to our house. How relieved I was after all those miles, a bad snowstorm, and being apart from our little girls for so long that we were all back together at home once again! I am sure my happiness and joy lasted for days.

According to my calculations, we drove a total of 7,335 miles on our trip. Cost for gas fill ups were $13.00, $11.00, $12.25, $9.00, $8.20, to give some examples back in 1978. That was for a Chevy suburban. The motel in Wyoming was a Best Western for $27.00. Another one was $19.50, and two nights at the Sands in San Luis Potosi was only $21.00. When we took the Munoz family out for supper, the total cost was $29.30 for eight people. So just some lists of costs which were so reasonable back then in Mexico. Prices in the States were much better also. We were gone for 22 days, and once again we were thankful God watched over us all that time and over so many miles of travels.

I think our *guardian angels* were there each mile of the way guiding and protecting us in all ways. Also, as a family, while we were apart from one another, *angels* were watching over our little girls also. Revelation 5:11 reads, "Then I looked and heard the voice of many angels, numbering thousands upon thousands, and ten thousand times ten thousand. They encircled the throne and the living creatures and the elders." What a comfort that not only is God always watching over us, but His *mighty angels* are watching over each one of us who believe and accept God in our lives.

LITTLE ANGELS AND MIGHTY ANGELS

After seeing the great needs of many people in Mexico, on our subsequent trips we always would pack our suburban with good used clothing to pass out to the people. We would have tracts in Spanish to pass out, always a big supply of pencils for the children, some candy and gum, good used toys, and school supplies. When our church people heard that we were making another trip to Mexico, many chipped in and made donations, and it was always easy to fill up our suburban.

As I wrote about this long trip, I cannot believe that we were gone for so long and I had to leave my little ones! Looking back, that was terrible. How did I ever do it? I know it certainly was not easy for me. I mentioned this to my husband last night while eating our supper. I said, "How did you ever talk me into taking such a long trip and being away from my little children for so long?" He said, "Looking back, did it hurt them any?" I guess maybe not at that young age. I do remember with our third daughter at almost three years, it did affect her when we left her with the Chicago cousins. After we picked her up and she was home again, she was very apprehensive for at least a year about being left behind again. She had to have me reinforce over and over that I would be back to get her, even when leaving her for a short time. My husband looks at it this way . . . look at all the trips and vacations over the years that we were able to take, and look at all the things we could do and see. Many husbands and wives do not have those opportunities.

To summarize a bit on our trips, we did several driving trips to California and spent time with my sister Darlene, her husband Richard, and daughter Amy. Dick and I visited by ourselves sometimes---and one time we flew out and brought my mom along after Dad had passed away. Richard and Darlene were always so good about hosting us even though with our family, all of a sudden, there were six extra people in their apartment. But they put up with us and always showed us a good time. One time when Dick had a work-related convention to go to in San Francisco, we were able to fly from there to Hawaii. We stayed with Dick's cousins and used their car which helped cut down on expenses. We also did several trips to Canada and one to Montana to see our friends. There were trips to the Smoky Mountains and the southern states. For a couple very special events, we went to the historic, famous, and magnificent Grand Hotel on Mackinac Island (Michigan). I will always treasure the many jaunts and the memories that were made. The beauty of God's creation was so evident on our trips.

With lots of traveling, it included many, many miles on the highways. God kept us safe over the many miles, protecting us from harm and danger. I recall one incident, however, on one trip in the middle of the night in which we faced a little dilemma. We had seven people in our seven passenger van, returning from a trip out west. Our oldest daughter was driving, and I was the copilot to make sure she did not fall asleep. A semi-truck was passing alongside us in the passing lane. He was almost completely past us when all of a sudden, we heard a crash and the tinkling of glass. Whether the semi threw up a stone while passing us, or he was too close and a strap or something from his truck hit us, but our huge window on the left side of our van broke (right behind the driver). Thankfully, no one was in that seat at the time since a couple people were lying on the floor sound asleep. The truck kept going unaware that anything had happened. We pulled off at the next exit and found a small gas station. But how do you fix a huge window like that to keep out the wind and to keep us warm? I had a sheet along, and we bought all the duct tape that the gas station had and taped the sheet in place. It looked pretty funny to finish our trip with our window looking like that. But we were thankful no one was in the seat at the time so no one was hurt by flying pieces of glass.

And there were the many Mexico trips . . . a trip once a year for six years straight. We skipped a year or two and then took some more trips to Mexico. Dick also flew down many times with his brother-in-law, Ben, and they often would take a couple other guys and do work projects at the children's home. Dick tried to add up all the times he went to Mexico, and he thinks it was pretty close to 20 times (maybe a dozen times for me). I mentioned earlier that he went down with a mission group in 1972, before we were married, fell in love with the country and the people, and made many close friends. It was a good place to travel inexpensively. We liked traveling in Mexico due to the ever changing scenery. We would see little brick houses or grass huts, herds of sheep and goats, cows and donkeys cross the road, beautiful mountain drives (with no guard rails!), not-so-beautiful desert roads, and lots of scattered and interesting little towns along the way where you got glimpses of how people lived. After being in Mexico, you always came away feeling so appreciative of our lives in the U.S.! We saw so many homes with no power, no sewer systems, no running water, people with few clothes, not much to eat . . . very poor! They would not be able to figure us Americans out with all our luxury conveniences and wasteful living. Yet, to visit these people is something you do not forget as they always gave you a royal welcome and were so friendly. When you visited at a church or in the homes, you were greeted with a handshake by all, even the littlest of children. Anyway, I feel you always came away a better person after traveling about in Mexico.

Something a bit surprising and different . . . the trip to Mexico in August 1973 found Dick, Ben, and friend Jesse helping out for most of the day at the children's home butchering a cow and two pigs. A lot of hard work, but they found it interesting also. We ladies had the unique experience of washing our clothes in a huge metal cylinder drum that rotated. It was homemade and worked well for the large amount of clothing from all the children at the orphanage. We had to hang the clothes outside on lines to dry.

An interesting story from one of our Mexico trips was when we boarded the cruise ship *Fair Sea* that had docked in Puerto Vallarta. A rather unique, friendly lady offered to take us aboard and we accepted. We rode in a shuttle boat to get out to the ship, as it was docked quite a ways out on the ocean. We ate lunch with her on the ship (for free) and had a little tour. I was afraid the ship would take off, and we would have no way to get back to shore (too far to swim!). This was illegal, we found out later---to go on a ship like that, but there was no security that stopped us. We also saw the *Pacific Princess* docked in Puerto Vallarta, and it was so close, we could have touched it. This boat was used in "The Love Boat," a popular ABC TV show that ran from 1977 to 1986.

On one of our trips in Mexico I was brave enough to go on my first (and last) parasail ride. Dick did, too, the day before. Parasailing is the big kite-like canopy, similar to a parachute that is pulled behind a motorboat---and in this case, on the ocean. I was harnessed in and had a little cord to pull when they signaled from WAY DOWN on the beach to pull the cord to bring me down. All was well and good while I was parasailing and I thought it was rather fun---EXCEPT I was up a little longer than planned! They had a problem with the other rider who was up at the same time as me, and he went down in the ocean when their boat ran out of gas. I sure was glad I was not behind that boat! I saw it all happen as I was way, way up in the sky! I would have been scared to death to be floating around in the ocean with fear of approaching sharks! Plus, it took a long time to bring that person in as they had to swim out to the boat with a gas can, and then go pick the person up.

Last night I asked my husband what memories stood out to him about some of the Mexico trips. Dick said his foremost memory was when he had the unique experience in the state of Oaxaca of visiting a magnificent ornate cathedral designed and built centuries ago by the Spaniards and based on European Gothic style structures. Far off the main tourist roads, few Americans have the opportunity to experience its majestic beauty. I did not go along on this venture since I was six months pregnant and thought it best to stay back at the pastor's home. They had warned me that the roads were very bumpy. The evangelical pastor we were staying with had somehow managed an agreement with the priest of this cathedral to show Christian films, like *Pilgrim's Progress* by John Bunyan. They (the pastor and wife), Dick, and Les and Sandy, who were making this trip with us from our church, traveled by vehicle down almost impassable roads. Then they walked the final distance to join the priest and the local people who were not used to seeing films in this huge cathedral. There was no electricity, so it had to be shown using a generator. After the film, they were able to hand out many Bibles and Christian literature in this truly ecumenical service---almost unheard of at this time in the history of the Catholic church in southern Mexico.

Following the long service with the time getting late, the women from the church planned on serving them, their guests, a dinner. The group wanted to decline but dared not offend them since the meal was already on the table waiting. Dick remembers in particular being served chicken soup as part of the meal. Sandy noticed chicken feet floating in her soup and tried to mask her astonishment and shock! Dick thinks that no part of that chicken was wasted and maybe they thought the feet added to the flavor. They did their part as guests and enjoyed and gave their thanks to the hosts for serving them.

Dick also mentioned the few times we went to the big city of Guanajuato. This city attracts many tourists because of its museum with naturally mummified bodies. There was a cholera epidemic in 1833, and they had to quickly bury many bodies in one huge grave. Much later, the corpses were discovered to be mummified. Scientists claim that the unique soil composition, weather with low humidity, and being 6,000 feet above sea level kept the bodies from decomposing. Of the 120 corpses found, 59 are on display. Guanajuato is also a very beautiful, large city with tree-lined streets, quaint plazas, and colorful buildings . . . a nice place to see and visit.

Another adventure that stuck out in Dick's mind was when we were visiting the children's home in San Luis Potosi. The administrator suggested we visit a pastor friend's church for the Sunday service. Juan Carlos grew up in the children's home and became a pastor. We kept in touch with him over the years, so we wanted to hear him preach and visit his church. They had a lot of rain previously, but we set out for this distant village. However, to our dismay and consternation we encountered many puddles on the not-so-well-traveled road. A couple puddles were very long and very deep! Our poor rental van went through water up to the bottom of the doors. I thought for sure the van was going to die right in the middle of the biggest puddle, and then what would we do! Somehow we made it through, and we did not encounter any engine troubles from the van getting wet. Otherwise, it was a good Sunday and a nice service, and the ladies of the church even prepared a good lunch for all of us. We had the opportunity to go around the village handing out lots of pencils, school supplies, used clothing, and some small toys.

Mexico's wealthier people shop in modern stores, and the poorer class shop at open-air markets. To walk through these busy markets is an experience in itself. Many smells (some unpleasant) assail you as you are walking through. The not-so-good smells are often from butchered chickens, slabs of beef, pork, and other cuts of meat hanging out in the open for who knows how long (and with flies buzzing on them liberally). And this is hard to believe, but we have seen it at more than one market---dead rats for sale. I guess perhaps the poorest of the poor buy something like that for some meat.

The same lady that found the chicken feet in her soup [Sandy] had quite a scare when we were back in the U.S. We made it through the border crossing procedure all right, and Sandy was taking a turn at driving. We were maybe 20 miles from the border when she came to a place where two uniformed men pulled us over, and one was pointing a machine gun at Sandy as she rolled down her window. Dick tried to converse with them in his limited Spanish! The best he could figure out was they were checking to make sure we did not have a stowaway. They only opened the back and moved a couple things, and then we could be on our way again. It took us all a while to breathe our sighs of relief after we faced those machine guns!

On our return trip from Mexico in February of 1984, we brought one of our pastor friend's sons back with us for a visit (from San Luis Potosi). Dick thought it would be really special for him to spend some time in the United States and to stay with us for a while. He offered it to the oldest son, but David decided he did not wish to go. Luis, at 15 years old, said he would like to go with us. We had to get special papers for him to go to the U.S., and the administrator at the children's home helped with the difficult procedure. Then on our way home, when we had to go through the border crossing in Laredo, there was trouble. They were not going to let him cross. After a lot of deliberation, they sent Dick and Luis over to another official, and he agreed to let him go to the U.S. Dick always said it was God's will that the official let him cross the border because all odds were against it.

So our children had an older brother around for five weeks (the girls were 9, 7, 5, and 3 years at the time). We had a couch bed in the front room so that became a temporary bedroom for Luis. At first, when Dick had to go to work and the kids were off to school, it was a bit awkward at home with Luis and me with our language barrier (I could not speak any Spanish, and Luis very little English). But he soon made friends with a Mexican family, and he would spend some days now and then with them. Plus, he got a job washing cars across the street at the local car dealership. He could do this whenever he was free, and he really appreciated this. He earned two dollars an hour which was a lot more than he could have made at most jobs in Mexico. While at our house, he experienced many new things like sledding, snowmobiling, bowling, visiting our Christian school, and eating our types of food. We tried to take him to see a lot while he was visiting. We went up north across the Mackinac Bridge, to Tahquamenon Falls, and the Soo Locks. Dick took him for a ride on a ski lift, and also flying in a small plane with my brother-in-law. We took him to the Grand Rapids malls, the museum, and the zoo. Luis could sing and play guitar, which he did at Newman Chapel and at our church in New Era. When it was time for him to return home, we brought him to Chicago and took him to the Museum of Science and Industry and the Sears Tower. Then Luis was put on a direct flight from O'Hare Airport to Mexico City where his father was going to meet him. All in all it was quite the experience for him and for us, and he was sad when he had to leave. We always wondered if it was something that benefited him or instead made him dissatisfied with his way of life, and maybe he yearned for more of the opportunities and luxuries that he had experienced in the United States.

 We had more adventures in Mexico, but I will move on. As I was thinking how God was watching over us during our many trips, I remembered a song that talks about whether upon the land or on the rolling sea, and day by day, our Father watches over us. He takes care of the flowers, trees, birds, butterflies, eagles, animals, and all things He created---and surely He watches over us. I have some thoughts about God's bountiful care in the devotional I wrote:

> I believe if we are wholeheartedly, sincerely, and conscientiously striving to live the life God wants us to live---it will be a great comfort to know He is always with us---watching over us and caring for us. Yes, we fail and stumble as imperfect human beings, but He will pick us up and help us start over in another new day, plus give us the strength to carry on! Our mistakes can become lessons for us, helping us to grow and mature. These lessons can help us to take steps forward and to do better the next time. We read in Psalm 33:13-15, "From Heaven the Lord looks down and SEES ALL mankind; from His dwelling place HE WATCHES all who live on earth---He who forms the hearts of all, who considers everything they do." And verse 18, "But the EYES OF THE LORD are on those who fear Him, on those whose hope is in His unfailing love." I hope this is a comfort to you today (as it is to me) as you travel along life's way.

FEARFUL TIMES, KIDS' SAYINGS, SNOWMOBILING

"When you pass through the waters, I will be with you; and when you pass through the rivers, they will not sweep over you. When you walk through the fire, you will not be burned; the flames will not set you ablaze. For I am the Lord, your God, the Holy One of Israel, your Savior " (Isaiah 43:2-3).

When we had two little children, I thought I was busy; then number three came along, and I never seemed to be able to keep up with everything anymore. They kept me busy and hopping most of the time! There were moments of frustration, but the girls sure were a joy and a pleasure, and we were so thankful to the Lord for them! Dick was still involved in many meetings and activities, and we were busy a lot of evenings, so the kids were getting used to that also. Often at suppertime the routine question from one daughter was "What will we be doing after supper, Daddy?"

In February of 1978, we bought the large two story home that we had rented for over four years after we were first married. Being owners instead of renters, we now had a lot of fixing up we wanted to do. First, we had Sears put up a nice fence for the kids, which was desperately needed since we lived right on a busy road (US Highway 31). They had a nice play area, and I got my wish for a clothesline outdoors, so I could have the nice smell of clothes dried out in the fresh air. I did a lot of painting---the garage and outdoor trim on the house windows (on the very high upstairs windows too!). Soon we remodeled the living room with many hours of hard work. Throughout the succeeding years, we did a lot of projects to update our old home and make it more comfortable and cozy. New Era is a nice, small, peaceful town, and we have been happy and content living here all our married lives.

Thinking back to the busy, child-rearing years when the kids were little, how relieved I am that worse things did not happen. I recall a few fearful times and some close calls. Once, a daughter was very sick with a high fever. Her temperature would go up to 103 degrees, and then return almost to normal the next day. The following day up to 104 degrees and then down again. We thought she was doing okay, so we left her at my folks and went to a basketball game one night. When we picked her up after the game, she was burning up! At home we took her temperature and it was 106 degrees, as high as the thermometer went! We called the doctor yet at midnight, and he said to give her cool baths and aspirin; we got her to sleep at 1:15 a.m. In the morning her temp was a little under 105, so again Dick gave her a cool bath, and she finally looked like she felt a bit better. By that night, it was down to 97 degrees. However, the next morning it shot back up to 105, and we called the doctor again. Finally, the next couple of days she improved except for a runny nose. I will never forget that incident, and I felt so guilty leaving her and going to a basketball game after

I found out how sick she was. She had quite a time of it and was a very sick little girl! She was so weak after that sickness; she would shake and wobble when she first tried standing. Our poor little girl! As parents we look back when things like that happened and wonder if we made the proper decisions. You try to do the right thing, but there is sometimes the guilt that is part of parenthood.

June 19, 1980, another scare and a night Dick and I well remember. This involved our third daughter, Nichole, who was 14 months old at the time. She woke up with a fever in the morning and did not feel well all day. I just figured it was one of those usual off days that kids get from time to time, so I gave her Tylenol a couple times for the fever, rocked her, and gave her lots of fluids. I did not even take her temperature; I knew she was hot, but I was giving her fluids and watching her closely. Later, Nichole had slept a bit in bed and woke up crying. Dick got her and he said she had a couple slight convulsions, one in the bed and one in his arms. Looking back, I always wonder why we did not call or take her to the doctor right then! He was holding her and rocking her, so I went back to doing my supper dishes when all of a sudden, I heard her cry out in an awful loud, scary manner. I hurried back to the living room, and she was having another bad convulsion, and then she passed out. I tried to call the doctor, but I could not get through. Poor Nichole was still out! We decided the fastest thing to do would be to just rush her up to Shelby Hospital three and a half miles away. We were watching another boy at the time, who was only seven or eight, and hollered upstairs for him to watch our other two daughters, only 5 and 3 years old, and we took off. Anyway, our poor baby was unconscious all that time, and I was scared to death. I drove while Dick still held her . . .

went about 80 miles an hour. Dick had his finger in her mouth all this time to keep her from biting her tongue. By the time we got there and found a nurse, maybe about 20 minutes had elapsed. Her color was not good, lips were blue, she was so limp, and I could not even tell if she was still breathing. When I wrote these notes down in 1980, I wrote "I get all upset just thinking about it!" Parenting can definitely be scary!

Nichole came to on the table in the emergency room. Her temperature was 105, and they gave her an aspirin suppository there. Then they made arrangements for us to meet our doctor at the Hart hospital; so we drove to Hart, another six and a half miles away. Earlier, I had called my sister in town to go over and stay with the young children at our house. Our doctor decided to admit Nichole and keep her under observation for 24 to 48 hours. I stayed there with her the whole time. I did not want our baby to be so scared by being alone in the hospital. So I had a long night and a long day as she was not released until 8:00 Friday evening. It had happened about 7:00 on Thursday night. She had chest x-rays, blood tests, and other routine tests, and all was normal. Our doctor decided the high temperature caused the convulsion along with cutting four more teeth at once, and he thought her ears looked like they had an infection in them.

She slept well the first night at home. I slept pretty good too, but slept most of the night on the floor next to her crib. My emotions were drained over the whole thing; a lot goes through your mind during such an experience like that! From then on, we always had Tylenol on hand and a tongue depressor, but she never had another convulsion. This scary experience made me take a long look at each member of my family and think how very much they meant to me. How quickly the routine of everyday life can fall apart, and how good it was to come home again after those long 24 hours. We had so much to praise God for---that it was not anything more serious, and we could come home to our wonderful house again and to our regular routine. Yes, we had a very busy household, but the fast pace and sometimes even some chaos is a sign of a healthy family! After a couple days, Nichole started being our happy, normal, smiley little girl again---what a relief! The doctor examined her again and said her ears looked better, so probably a combination of ear infection and teething may have been the cause of the high temperature. Another instance of God's protection and *guardian angels* watching over us through that traumatic experience!

Another bit of a scare with Nichole happened when she was 17 months old and I neglected to put the car emergency brake on while I was unloading a few things. As a precaution, I normally did put the brake on when leaving a child in the car alone and removed the keys. Nichole was happily playing, so I was doing something quick with the hose behind the car when I heard a click, and the car started rolling backwards! Nichole had managed to pull the gear selector out of park. Thankfully, it was on the flatter part of our drive, and I could quickly hop in and stop it. Also, it was a very good thing I was outside at the time and not in the house, as the car could easily have rolled out onto Garfield Road. Who knows how far it would have kept going on Garfield Road with a hill! Perhaps it would have even rolled across the busy Highway 31! Also I was thankful that our second daughter, Kristi, was not playing behind the car when it started rolling, or she may have been hurt!

On a different morning a few weeks later, Nichole got a quarter caught in her throat and gave me a scare. Thankfully, a few hard pats on the back, and she coughed it out. She had been very good about not putting things in her mouth, and I had just told her not to put any money in her mouth. Kristi also gave me a frightening moment when she was three months old. I had gone to talk to Dick a minute in the other room while Kristi was in her infant seat in the kitchen. I walked back into the kitchen and Kristi was choking. I patted her hard on the back and up came three raisins! Her almost two-year-old big sister had put them in her mouth in that short time; she must have thought she should share.

One more scary and upsetting story about Nichole yet from some written notes about it on December 24, 1982:

> I am so relieved and happy to be home as a FAMILY this Christmas Eve! We went to Grand Rapids today to take our girls and two other boys to see the big malls and Christmas decorations. It was towards the end of the day, and I had Dick take the kids while I ran into one store to buy a couple little things yet for Christmas. When I met up with him again, he had to tell me that Nichole, 3 years old, and the 6-year-old, Clare, were missing! They had lingered behind when Dick assumed they were with him, and then they went the wrong way to catch up. They were lost 20 minutes to half an hour before we found them. I think I lost five years off my life since so many thoughts went through my mind, such as thinking someone ran off with them. Some nice lady had brought them to the information desk where we finally found them after some frantic searching. I guess the kids were not too worried, which is surprising knowing how

shy Nichole was. I was shaken up tremendously though! What a thing to have happen- - -it was very distressing and disturbing to me. All the way home, which was 70 miles, I kept thinking how thankful I was and how Christmas that year would be the best ever having our whole family together! It could have been much worse.

I do not think we had any more fearful times than most families. I am sure if you thought about it, you could come up with incidents of concern also that happened to you over the years. I will share a couple more of ours. This was a very alarming and harrowing one for us as parents and for the daughter that ran down the steps to tell us. We had some friends over for a visit, and our two oldest girls and their daughter were upstairs playing in the girls' bedroom. All of a sudden we heard a crash and our oldest daughter came down the stairs frantically crying---we had a hard time getting out of her what had happened since she was so terrified. She thought Kristi was dead! She finally told us that Kristi (three years old) had tried climbing up on the heavy, wooden bookcase to get something, and it fell over on her. She was caught underneath! Dick hurried upstairs and said it was a wonder that Kristi only got a scratch on her back out of it. Our oldest received a gash on her head where it must have hit her; the visiting girl was without an injury. We moved the heavy thing out of their room yet that night so it would never happen again. Dick said it was quite a sight when he ran upstairs and there lay the big, heavy old bookcase flat on the floor, and no Kristi to be seen. She was completely under it with not even an arm showing! This cabinet had four glass doors on it also, so the girls all sure could have been badly hurt. How Kristi was under that heavy thing without becoming injured was really something! So our conclusion: God sent a *guardian angel* to keep Kristi safe that night!

I think I better lighten things up a bit and mention some cute things the kids said when they were little. One came into the kitchen one night when I was fixing supper and said she did not like "shiver." I was fixing chili and she could not remember the name for it.

Our three and a half year old asked the question, "How does God make peoples?" One time we had left the girls at their grandparents' house and we went to pick them up. As we were ready to leave, I mentioned I hoped they were good for Grandpa and Grandma. Kristi said, "We were, but we cannot be good all the time!"

It was hard not to chuckle when Kristi prayed, "Bless the poor people who don't have any food *except rice*. She must have had a story about it in Sunday School. And it was funny when she once asked, "Do Spanish people laugh in Spanish?" But it was special when she would come to me and say, "You are the best Mom I have." There were also the words they twisted around like "hairplane" for airplane and "friger-freighter" for refrigerator.

Looking back and thinking of the child-rearing days, yes, they were so busy, but they were very special too. Do not ever wish those years away. Those days will go so fast when your children are infants and toddlers, and you cannot get those days back. When I think of my little girls who were close in age, I always say it would be nice to be able to go back in time and have my daughters as babies and toddlers once again, but only for a few weeks! It would be nice to be able to better remember the child-rearing days and how special they really were. The older we get, the harder it is to remember the happenings of 45 years ago. When you have a busy family, you need to be well organized and keep your priorities straight. I admit, I often had trouble with both of those things.

I have an illustration about priorities in the devotional book I wrote:

> Alicia and Dick hit a huge hawk today on the way to Muskegon. Alicia was driving, going right around 70 mph, when this huge hawk came swooping suddenly out of the sky hitting the right side of the windshield very forcefully! It is a wonder the windshield did not break! The hawk may have been diving for some little critter scurrying across the road and was so focused on its prey that it was unaware of a car coming down the expressway at 70 mph and thus, the larger danger for that careless hawk.
>
> We are often that way in life . . . so focused on the tiny, trivial things that we are not in tune and watchful for the hidden dangers and pitfalls that come along. Can it be that we are so focused on preparing meals, doing laundry, keeping a clean and tidy house [all good things] that we may miss when one of our children is lonely, depressed, or struggling in some area of his or her life? Or perhaps the father is so involved in church meetings, school functions, helping a neighbor [also all good things], but he does not have time at home for a child who looks up to him and is craving time alone with that parent. There are times when you have to learn to say "no" gracefully. When you are thinking of taking on another job ask yourself, "What will be its impact on our family life?" Learn to slow your pace. Let your children know you always have time for them. It is easy to become so involved with the everyday things of life

that we miss out on our times alone with God, miss quality time with young children, or miss the beauties of creation. We live in an extremely busy and complex world these days, and it is often very difficult to keep our priorities straight. We must strive each and every day to please God first and always. Do not be like the hawk and lose your focus on that which is most important as we walk down life's path! I like this prayer I found, and we should pray, "Turning to ourselves, Father, we need to improve in so many areas---we need to grow spiritually, need to grow in love, need more patience, need more zeal and energy to accomplish our various tasks, need better attitudes, need to be more willing, need to be more caring and concerned for others, need to make better use of our time, and need to be better, kinder, more gracious Christians. Help us, we pray with these needs. In Jesus name, Amen."

Snowmobiling is one of the activities we so appreciated and did a lot of over the years. When the children were too little to go, Dick's parents would often watch them so Dick and I could go. We stored our machines in their barn, so it was convenient to go from there and leave the kids with them. Many Saturdays they would watch the kids all day, allowing us to put on many miles riding snowmobiles. We often invited some young boys to go with us, and others with snowmobiles often joined us too for this fun sport. Of course, our girls at young ages started riding with us and then driving their own machines as well. Even now in 2022, when there is snow, we have two daughters and their spouses who do not live too far away and can join us for some Saturday rides. We continue to like snowmobiling and can still enjoy it together as a family.

LITTLE ANGELS AND MIGHTY ANGELS

"Michiganders" get to enjoy the change of seasons, and it seems the older I become, the more I enjoy the seasonal changes. Maybe because we have more time to enjoy the beauties of nature, or maybe our senses are enhanced as we age. I wrote once of a beautiful snowmobile ride describing the beauty of wintertime and quote:

> Our first snowmobile ride of the winter: a beautiful ride of 50 miles. It was one of those days when the snow covered trees, bushes, and branches---clumps of snow clinging to anything and everything, making the beauty indescribable, breathtaking, extraordinary, and marvelous! I call it one of God's blessings showing us His beauty in creation. You wonder how it is possible for those large clumps of snow to stay perfectly balanced on a twig or branch, or on the pine trees. It is so amazing! And there has been no wind or storms to blow it out of the trees and bushes. The snow keeps accumulating, building up, and making unusual shapes. There are numerous balls of snow of many different sizes, some six inch, eight inch, and even twelve inch balls, or dozens of balls on one branch or bush. God's creation and workmanship is unparalleled by anything else! I sat driving my machine down the trail looking at all this wondrous beauty! In a couple of the orchards that we went through, the lumps of snow hanging on a branch were at least a foot or more deep. How can snow pile that high [and wide too] on that narrow twig or branch? Only by God's special placement! If He knows every hair on our heads, He knows the placement and order of even the snowflakes as they fall and accumulate. Anyway, I enjoy the thrill of snowmobiling and I am thankful, too, for God's blessings today in the beauty of the newly fallen

snow. It was a beautiful picture to behold. And I enjoy the feeling of the breeze coming in under my face shield so fresh and invigorating. I just feel energized, vitalized, and refreshed as I sail, glide, skim, and cruise over the snow. Can you tell that I enjoy the sport? It is a nice thing to do as a family, and a wonderful way to see the beauty and handiwork of God in His creation. Otherwise, at our ages of 75 and 77, we would tend to stay in the warmth of our cozy home rather than venture out in the cold. Snowmobilers can enjoy the winter beauties like no one else can [except skiers and hikers], and I marveled at this beauty over and over again as we rode along in the undisturbed whiteness. We witnessed tree limbs hanging heavy with snow, creeks trickling along with pieces of floating ice, and snow-covered bridges. It is this beauty that cannot be seen from a traveled road or from a home. Sometimes you have hoarfrost too that sticks to all the bushes making it just like a winter wonderland. And the sun shining on everything making it glisten and sparkle. Or it is nice sometimes to shut off the snowmobile and enjoy the silence and see all the diamonds shining in the snow [sunlight hitting tiny ice crystals in the snow and reflecting the light].

When we would take younger boys along who were inexperienced, we had some mishaps. Once Dick had invited a 12-year-old boy along, and he snowmobiled into a six or so foot deep ditch (with some water in it) near the celery flats in Montague. He was following Dick on the trail and cut a corner short to catch up; he realized too late that there was a ditch on both sides of the trail, and he was heading for it. He got off in time or he might have really hit the windshield hard on impact and could have been seriously hurt. The snowmobile came out of it okay also with just a bunch of extra mud on it. We had to enlist the help of three men and several kids to get the snowmobile out again. It took a lot of shoveling, and they tied a cable on it so everyone could pull. What an experience!

One afternoon, Dick took five children snowmobiling, some who had never been snowmobiling before. One girl wanted to drive a little by herself, because she had taken a snowmobile class in school. Dick picked a nice wide open field to let her go around in a couple of times. Why she panicked on a side hill and opened the throttle near wide open, no one knows. But as a result, she headed straight for the woods, over a huge bank and flew with the machine airborne for about 15 feet! She hit the ground once and bounced another 10 feet in the air until she finally fell off the machine. You would have to see the place afterwards, as I did, to believe it. No one could have driven through the same place going probably 40 mph and miss several huge trees. Dick had visions of finding our machine wrapped around a tree totally wrecked with a young girl hurt critically or dead. Yet she was okay! Another case of God's protection perhaps using a *mighty angel* to watch over everyone!

Here is another story about a Saturday accident. This time we had two of my brothers and a niece riding with us. The niece had not ridden with us before, and she was a newer driver. She was doing just fine until we were riding on the crest of a very steep hill. The trail on top was very narrow---barely wide enough for the snowmobiles. We were riding slowly along, and I was following my niece when all of a sudden the left ski on her machine nicked a small stump of a tree that was sticking up.

It made her swerve, and she went down over the cliff. It scared me terribly, as it was a very tall, steep hill covered with trees. I hollered to her grandpa and uncle who were riding right behind me. They jumped off their machines and hurried down, worried that my niece might have hit a tree and be seriously hurt. She had fallen off the snowmobile, and her helmet was knocked off, but she was all right! She and the machine had landed about 12 to 15 feet down the steep incline with the machine banged up a little from hitting a tree. It still was driveable, but how to get it back up the hill---that was impossible! The only thing to do was perhaps ride the snowmobile on down the hill, but then it would have to be ridden up a very steep, long embankment to get up to the road. That looked impossible also, but my brother was willing to give it a try. We all watched apprehensively as he drove around trees going down the steep hill and then, giving it a lot of gas, he got past some smaller trees and brush, and tried to get through all the deep snow and up to the road. Thankfully, he made it on the first try, and we were able to resume our ride and make it home safely. Again, there were no cell phones back then to call for help. I imagine my poor niece saw trees coming at her in her sleep that night! But most of the time things went well on snowmobile rides with no problems. We were cautious drivers and enjoyed seeing the beauty of wintertime, feeling no need to fly down trails at high speeds.

A few more thoughts on snowmobiling from the devotional that I wrote:

> I sat on my snowmobile today and took the time to watch snowflakes swirling slowly to the ground. Two lessons I learned today: 1. A reminder to enjoy God's

creation---by taking time! Too often we are too busy to enjoy all the beauty around us! Today, I challenge you to look around and observe something unique and beautiful that you have not noticed before. It could be something as simple as a lovely blue sky and big, white fluffy clouds. 2. How insignificant one little snowflake may seem . . . but they do add up and sometimes to HUGE amounts. So the little things we do in life, no matter how small and insignificant, add up and DO make a difference! Just doing one act of kindness at a time can really add up just like one snowflake at a time! Make your day fulfilling and complete by scattering acts of kindness to your family, to friends, and to others whom you may come in contact with today. This will enhance and cheer up your day and make another person's day easier and brighter!

A quote that I read in a card once, "Some people miss the sunshine and live mostly in the shadows." I believe this is true, and I do not have a lot of empathy for people who go around with a long face, complaining, bored, are short tempered, and often restless. There is the saying, "Life is what you make it." I know, some have valid reasons when they are often down such as serious health issues, and that I understand. But for those who are bored and restless, "put your chin up" and find constructive things to do. There is no reason to be bored no matter your age. There are numerous ways a person can volunteer their help, visit the shut-ins, spread a little kindness and cheer, or find countless other rewarding things to do. Proverbs 15:15 says, "A miserable heart means a miserable life; a cheerful heart fills the day with song" (MSG---Message Bible).

We need to count our blessings more often and look at the bright side of things. We have so much to be thankful for and too often we take these things for granted . . . warm homes, family, loved ones, friends, abundance of food and clothing, freedom, security, our Christian schools and colleges, churches, the ability to work and play, health and strength, and God supplying our needs. We need to be happy and content with the simple and little things. If you do not feel you have many gifts or talents, you can always be caring, sympathetic, helpful and good, truthful, kind, and a good listener. Because we are so blessed, we should include thankfulness to God for how good He has been to us throughout the ages. Like our pastor said recently, we need an "attitude of gratitude!" A poem I wrote nearly 40 years ago ties in about God's blessings and goodness:

SO GOOD TO ME

God has been so good to me,
But a small glimpse is all I see.
I see all my material things,
What happiness this often brings.

But far deeper goes my wealth;
Far more important than even health;
Because if I soon should die
I would still have riches on high!

For there God is preparing a place
Because of His abounding grace.
Yes, a glimpse is really all I see,
But God surely has been good to me!

I really can't see all He's done,
And my thankfulness has just begun,
Because each moment of the day,
I'm going to search Him in a new way.

Seeking Him with all my heart
So His blessings will not depart.
By seeing His works anew,
A new awareness I will have too.

So earnestly I pray now dear God
As on the way I trod,
Only You will I see
Because You have been SO GOOD TO ME!

BUSY DAYS, FAMILY TRIP, BEAUTY OF NATURE

"Consider how the lilies grow. They do not labor or spin. Yet I tell you, not even Solomon in all his splendor was dressed like one of these" (Luke 12:27).

I mentioned earlier that God blessed us with a fourth daughter, born May of 1981. The following is from some notes I wrote at the time of her birth:

> Alicia almost had to be delivered by the two nurses and Dick as our doctor only made it by the "skin of his teeth." I blamed it on the nurses, as I had told them I would feel better if my doctor was present with the contractions coming fast and hard, but they figured there still was time. He only had time, however, to put on gloves and come rushing in all disheveled from being woken up out of his sleep. After a couple of minutes, we had another beautiful little girl! Birth is such a special thing for parents and even for grandparents. But as a mother . . . oh, the feeling of joy and thankfulness that wells up inside of you as you hold and feel your newborn baby in your arms. What a beautiful and perfect little baby God again has so wonderfully given us! To undress

her and see her perfect little form, tiny legs, and red little feet stretching out- - -what a miracle new life is! I am so very happy and thankful! I love to watch her little expressions and her pretty, dark eyes. I love her so much already! How special to let it seep in after our wait of nine months, that our new little one is finally here to join our family!

It was pretty unique that the same doctor delivered all four of our daughters and our pastor friend baptized them all. We were married in an odd-numbered year, and the girls were born every other year after that, in odd-numbered years. We called Alicia our surprise baby. We kept her birth a secret from Dick's sister and husband in Germany until her husband was out of the army. Dick's parents and another sister and husband had gone to Germany to see them, and they had to keep it a secret also. In fact, Alicia was born while they were there on that trip. Dick's parents called from Germany maybe a week after the due date (when the sister and husband were not around) to find out if it was a boy or a girl, and the name. That was such a fun surprise when they came home a couple months later, and they had another niece that they knew nothing about!

I was older when I had number four, and I wrote this down about that busy time:

> I am emotional, tired a lot, and things seem overwhelming. I just need to hang in there. The children grow up so fast and then, sadly, I will never be able to enjoy this facet of our lives again. Time is so short---I need to enjoy and try not to worry and get so easily frustrated. But It was not surprising that

I would have trouble dealing with things with four little ones and maintaining a household when I was not getting enough sleep at night. After Alicia started to sleep longer during the nights, and I got more sleep and rest, things improved. After almost four weeks, I felt more confident about having to watch all four little children again. Things were looking up even though it was still a bit overwhelming with all of the work that there always was. I totally loved my four little girls, but I did get weary caring for them, and it was so easy to get caught up in all the busyness. As I got older, I did not always have as much energy to keep going. I was pretty busy from the time I got up to the time the last one was tucked safely into bed at night. A typical day for me was to get up at 6:30 a.m. and to stay very busy with children, laundry, housework, cooking, dishes, and getting kids ready for bed until 9 p.m. I used to try and get an hour of quiet and relaxation while the kids were napping or resting in the afternoon in order to keep a good frame of mind.

Then I wrote this down once when I felt so overwhelmed with busyness in 1982:

> It is one of those days when I need to jot a few things down to express my feelings. I just feel depressed when I have my goals for my days, but I cannot seem to even begin to live up to them. Somehow I need a better schedule, or cannot let it bother me when I do not succeed. I need strength and guidance in this child-raising, as I often feel such a failure. I need to try harder to keep my priorities in order, first things first, and not let it bother me when I just cannot get it all accomplished. I need to do the best I can and then not

worry about it. So I pray You will help me today with my attitude . . . help me to look on the bright side of things. So many people have real problems and concerns. Our problems look so small compared to theirs.

Some young mothers may be feeling frustrated also with being too busy. God knows our every thought . . . and it can be comforting that God knows when you feel inadequate to meet the day-to-day challenges. He knows when you feel defeated and like a failure, and He knows your heart's desires.

Here we were, entering the very busy phase of our life with four young children. I felt when we had two little ones, my life was very busy. When we had three, I seemed to always be behind in everything. By the time number four came along, it did not matter---I was already very busy, one more just went with the flow of things. Plus, I was entering a new chapter in my life, sending the first child off to school. I remember it gave me a funny feeling knowing my first little girl would be gone all the time during the school week. She was getting more independent and out from under "mommy's wings." But we were busy and always did a lot in the evenings---riding our Solex bikes (mopeds) with a couple of the girls in seats behind and a couple at grandparents or with a babysitter. We often went visiting or had company over, and also spent time with both sets of parents. There were not many evenings that we just stayed at home. Dick was often on the council at church or on the school board, and taught Sunday School. I was involved at the school's fundraiser society and went to a Bible study. Dick still made runs with our suburban to pick up kids for Newman Chapel. Every Monday night he put on a good 60 miles to bring boys to and from the boys' club at the New Era

Christian Reformed Church, and on alternate Mondays picked up the girls for Calvinettes (about 18 to 20 would pile into our vehicle). And for many years, I drove a school bus to pick up the children for summer Vacation Bible School at Newman Chapel. When our girls were old enough, they attended Vacation Bible School, and the younger ones rode the bus with me or stayed with Grandma and Grandpa. Maybe all the busyness kept us young. I tried to keep a balance in our life and have plenty of time for our young children also. It is important in child-rearing years that we are not too busy to enjoy the wonderful family God has given us. We should not get so caught up in the whirlwind of life that we forget to be thankful to Him for our children, homes, churches, Christian schools, luxuries, and the great country in which we live. A guest minister preached on Psalm 23:2-3, "He makes me lie down in green pastures, He leads me beside quiet waters, He restores my soul." We often get too busy with "things" in life. There comes a time when God wants us to lie down in the green pastures, slow down for the purpose of renewing and restoring our souls and minds. The green pastures are a place of comfort; slow down and listen to God's still, quiet voice. When we do this, it will make us more energized and invigorated to carry on the tasks that are before us.

Doing things together as a family was important in those early years (and later years). For many years in a row, we would do the annual bridge walk across the Mackinac Bridge. When the kids were babies or toddlers, we pushed them in strollers; they have many bridge walk certificates. One year, when the girls were older, they even walked the bridge with President George Bush, Sr. Our girls were some of the first ones on the bridge after the President (and all the people that accompanied him). No one was allowed to walk right with him, but they could catch a glimpse of him once in a while during the walk and when he gave a short speech at the end. That was a lot of fun for them. Several times on these trips we went farther north to see beautiful Tahquamenon Falls in upper Michigan. A few times we also took a boat to Mackinac Island and enjoyed most of the day there. Summers consisted of the usual swimming lessons, some camping, dealing with swimmers itch, lots of time at the lake or in pools, and picnics.

A daughter was watching some of our family videos the other night. She reminded me that she saw how we often took other kids with us on our excursions. The one she watched was when we went to John Ball Zoo in Grand Rapids (70 miles away). We had about five extra kids plus our own four, and so she wondered how we kept track of them all! I do not remember, but I think all the kids were pretty good about staying with us as a group. The video also showed a bunch of the kids on the floor in the back of the suburban playing games together. Those were the days before seat belt requirements in the back. My husband often invited other children along, so our vehicle was often packed with kids going with us to one event or the other.

Somehow during all this busyness, I found a new hobby or interest. I discovered I liked making things with wood. I never took any classes; I just learned by doing. The summer Alicia was born, I made a large red bridge for the kids in their fenced-in play area. Then I had another big idea and after four days of very intense work and long hours, I produced the finest tree house in all of New Era (maybe!). When the girls had their friends over, they often enjoyed eating their lunches on the table up in the tree house and playing up there. Prior to these two items, I made a large, pretty red fence (with flowers in front) that divided the garden from the lawn. This idea of the fence was inspired by seeing one that I liked at a house in a town four miles away. One day I stopped and told the lady I wanted to build a fence like hers, and she let me take some pictures. It took me quite a while to build the long fence, but it lasted for many years. I never considered myself a very crafty person, since I did not knit, crochet, or sew any more than I had to, but I guess I had some creativity with my woodworking projects. I made a go-kart for the kids and also did a few projects in the house, such as a window seat and a loft with a ladder in Kristi's room. Over the years I also did lots and lots of painting and wallpapering in our older home.

When our littlest daughter turned two, the high chair could finally be put in the attic after almost eight years of continuous use. She could now just use a booster chair. Soon there were no more diapers to change, no more bottles to feed, no babies to rock, but I was still very busy and often I did not get a chance to sit and relax until 9:30 p.m. By then, I was so tired I would just go to bed also. But I dearly, dearly loved my family and would not trade the job of motherhood for anything else in the whole world! How amazing and wonderful to watch our little children grow and learn to crawl, to walk, and then to talk and become their own little persons with unique personalities and characteristics. What a responsibility and obligation God has entrusted to us as parents to care for and nurture our little ones, and to guide them as they become older.

When the girls were 2, 4, 6, and 8, we decided to take a family trip to California. This was quite an undertaking with the girls being so young, but they could bring a lot of toys along as we had room in our full-size van. They brought along plenty of stuff to help keep themselves occupied. I tried to think of things to help too. I read about this idea once and implemented it. I fixed up a man's long sleeve shirt and hung it up in the back of the van. I had little wrapped gifts pinned in the folded sleeves, in the pockets, and in various places on the shirt that the girls could take turns opening once each day. The girl opening the gift would pass out the items to her siblings---little toys, gum, crayons, small candies, and just a bunch of little treats that they could look forward to opening each day. I also had a big list of printed rules hanging up in the back of the vehicle like: "Don't be too loud in the car," "No fighting or arguing," "Obey Daddy and Mommy," and "Be kind and helpful."

For long trips we always brought along our homemade GORP. The girls looked forward to when they could snack on this. I would fill up a little container for each one of them. We enjoyed GORP as a family, and I still bring it for just Dick and me on trips. Just now I asked my tablet what GORP stood for, as I never knew for sure. The answer was "Good Ol' Raisins and Peanuts," a trail mix used by hikers. But you can make it up any way you wish. We often used Cheerios, Lucky Charms, peanuts, chocolate chips, peanut butter chips, M & M peanuts, and plain M & M's. It certainly was cheaper than buying snacks at gas station stops.

The following is a recap from my trip diary about the California trip:

> We left on our first family trip January 29 at 4:53 a.m. That was a pretty good departure time with getting all the kids up, and the house secured and shut up by

that early hour. The first eventful happening, about three hours into the trip, was that Alicia got sick. But thankfully, it did not last long . . . just a little motion sickness, I guess. We stopped in St. Louis and went up the Arch---a first time for the girls and me. It was fun and interesting but a little too confining for me. It is really something how they could build such a great and unusual structure, very beautiful! It is made of stainless steel and is 630 feet above the ground.

Then on and on we drove . . . ALL night, because that is when we made our best time. The girls all slept the whole night through, so we did not have to stop at restrooms. Night is a good time to travel with four little ones. The next day, Sunday, we stopped in Albuquerque, New Mexico and took the kids up on the tram, the largest in the world. That is just fantastic to go from the warmth up to the snow at 10,360 feet. The air was so cool and crisp; there was such beautiful and awesome scenery. There were lots and lots of skiers so we watched them for a while. Albuquerque is known for its balloonists and hang gliders. They were bringing two hang gliders up when we were waiting for our ride down, but we did not get to watch any come off the mountain. A couple daughters felt a little faint from the great change in elevation. We arrived at our destination in Rehoboth, New Mexico about 5 p.m. Dick, and the two older girls, still had time to make it to church after a quick supper in the dining room.

We had a good night of sleep after getting to bed nice and early. The girls were still on Michigan time and woke up about 5 a.m. Monday morning was spent letting the two older girls visit 2nd grade and Kindergarten at school with the Navajo Native Americans. Dick and I toured the grounds and became more acquainted with the Christian Reformed Church work at Rehoboth. We ate lunch with close to 300 students and afterwards drove to Zuni to see the Christian Reformed Church's work there. It is a very poor area but you can buy silver and turquoise jewelry of the finest quality there [the girls and I bought some]. We ate supper again with the students and retired early.

The kids woke up again at 5:30 a.m. so we had plenty of time to pack up before our 7:00 a.m. breakfast at the school's dining room. We drove out of Gallup and into Arizona enjoying the pretty scenery. Kids are busy playing and are too young to really enjoy the sights. They do travel well though, keeping occupied with all the things they brought along. Three things we experienced to remind us of God's watchful care over us and His protection so far:

1. Dick accidently ran a stop light in St. Louis but no traffic was coming!
2. In Rehoboth, the outside storm door stuck when I went to the car to get something, and Nichole and Alicia were alone in the bathtub in the apartment. I finally managed to open the door after pulling it with a lot of force!
3. Dick almost backed into a car that had pulled in right behind him in a parking spot at the Grand Canyon.

We had a full day of changing sights . . . we went through huge mountains with lots of snow, then rolling plains and deserts without snow and barren land, through forest land, the Petrified Forest, and then to the Grand Canyon. It was a beautiful, clear day and the Grand Canyon was as spectacular as ever! The canyon is 277 miles long and averages 18 miles in width. It measures 5,700 feet deep at the North Rim. We did not cover many miles today, but we saw so many beautiful and interesting sights. I am convinced you cannot enjoy the immense beauty of the Grand Canyon doing only one day stops with little glimpses. You need to spend a couple of days there and go down into the canyon itself on donkeys or hike down, except I am not brave enough for that. It would be enjoyable to see the sunsets down there when the rays of the sun bring out all the hidden beauty of the many colored rocks. I always feel a bit cheated with a one-day peek because I know there is so much more beauty and wonder in the canyon.

The girls are really doing well. Alicia is especially surprisingly good at two and a half years and will sit for so long quietly on our laps [before the days of required seat belts]. She plays nicely with her toys for long periods at a time and sleeps so good nights. She has adjusted well. We stayed in a small, dirty town called Williams tonight after leaving the Grand Canyon.

We woke up early again at 5:00 a.m., had breakfast at Denny's, and were on the expressway by 7:30 a.m. Now we are riding along in desert territory with surrounding mountains. We crossed into California at 9:00 a.m. their time. We lost our last four apples at the inspection point, because Dick was honest and said we had some. Next, we arrived in Palm Springs; it was raining, so the area looked drab and dreary, not at all pretty which it really is. We drove through more rain and even a bit of snow on our way to Los Angeles, which probably almost never happens in that desert country. Sadly, we ended up in the rush-hour traffic and did not make it to Richard and Darlene's [my sister and husband] until about 5:30 p.m. It seemed good to finally go to bed that night.

My folks had flown out to spend time with Richard and Darlene, so they were there the same time we were for part of the time. On Thursday, my dad, Dick, and Richard took off for the morning. They saw the Queen Mary from the shore [they did not take the tour] and rode around sight-seeing. My mom, the girls, and I stayed home and I did a load of laundry. Then we met Darlene at her office, and she introduced us to some of her co-workers. Darlene took us out to a cafeteria to eat. It was a bit challenging to get all the girls settled cafeteria style. In the process of helping the girls, poor Darlene spilled a plate of spaghetti and meatballs all over when it slipped out of her hands. She had spaghetti all over her nylons, on my purse, and some on my pants. It was just something that could not be helped. Next we brought the kids back for naps, and Dick washed and thoroughly cleaned the van. Later my dad and the rest of us went to the ocean for a while. We saw people surfing in their wetsuits, and the kids had fun looking for shells. They could find lots of interesting things because so much had washed ashore from some recent storms. At night we took a little ride up a mountain to see all the pretty lights down in the city below.

We went to Disneyland all day on Friday. The girls had such an exciting and fantastic time! Something that happened at Disneyland that my dad did not like us telling . . . we were so careful to make sure we did not lose the four little girls in the big crowds of people, and then the only one who got lost was my dad! He went to find a candy bar for my mom, became mixed up in his directions, and walked all over the place! Dad was tired out when he finally found us, and Mom never did get her candy bar! After such a busy day, everyone was very tired and bed felt so good once again!

It was a rainy day on Saturday, but we still left about 9:00 a.m. and rode around until about 5:00 p.m. First, we followed the ocean north and saw damage from the storms. A road was washed out and lots of mud had slid down along the road that workers were clearing away. Next, we came to a cute place called Santa Claus Lane with lots of unique shops. Santa Barbara was nearby, a beautiful town where we ate at a good restaurant. We took a real long drive through the mountains on some winding roads and saw some beautiful orange groves. There were other kinds of orchards and a huge dam---a lovely ride. We returned home and had a nice ham supper. After supper Richard took us on another tour of the city.

Sunday morning we went to the 9:30 a.m. service at the Garden Grove's Crystal Cathedral. Our seats were in the second row in the front, right by the huge organ. I was impressed with the beauty of the church---all the glass, plants, fountains, and I even saw a bird flying around way up in the top. The bird was singing its heart out along with the choir and the magnificent organ. Then we took a tour of the Queen Mary. It is so huge with lots to see; we could easily have spent a whole day there instead of just a few hours. Once my mom, with some other ladies, flew to California and stayed a couple nights on the Queen Mary when they attended a ladies' retreat.

We arrived back at Darlene's apartment about 3:30 p.m., and had to get things organized so Dad, Mom, Darlene, and her daughter, Amy, could watch our girls. I went with Dick to Los Angeles for a Canning Company Convention that was related to his work, and he had to attend. I stayed with him Sunday night, and he took me out to one of the best downtown restaurants at the

Bonaventure Hotel. That was fun! We walked around awhile looking over the hotel . . . a very beautiful and unusual structure. I really did not feel safe in it, though, with all of its pillars of cement and the way it was constructed. I was perfectly fine with staying in another motel overnight! Later we had room service, and I had a delicious, huge hot fudge sundae in addition to my big meal at the hotel; fun to splurge once!

I was up early, had breakfast with Dick, and then I took the car back to Richard and Darlene's apartment. We hurried around and got the kids ready, and we all rode along to bid farewell to my folks at the airport. It was a bit sad for Darlene, since it would be a while before she saw the folks again. We went back to the apartment, Darlene went to work, we had a quick lunch, and I put some tired kids down for naps. It was a rainy day so a good day to catch up on laundry and other things at the apartment. I fixed supper and afterwards Darlene took the girls and me to the huge mall in Santa Monica. The girls got to choose a couple things to buy at a real cute shop. Back to Darlene's again, and we fell wearily into bed.

Dick is still at his convention. Today turned out to be a beautiful warm day, so I took the girls to the Los Angeles Arboretum east of Pasadena. We sure enjoyed the nice day. The girls liked seeing the peacocks, ducks, birds, waterfalls, and little lakes. They had fun hiking down the jungle trail, seeing the old train depot, Queen Anne's cabin, and the many gardens. Such a pretty place with its 127 acres of trees, shrubs, flowers, and greenhouses. Next, we took a ride over to where I used to live on Buena Vista street in Duarte only ten miles away. I showed the girls my old apartment complex and pool, and Santa Teresita Hospital where I had worked. It brought back lots of memories; my girlfriend and I sure had it good when we lived there! What a nice area to live, so close to the mountains, and we had two years to enjoy it. I tried to locate my boss, Sr. Francis, as I would have liked to see her once again, but she was not working there at the hospital anymore.

We headed back to Darlene's apartment and went out to a good pizza restaurant for supper. Later, after getting some groceries, I mistakenly locked the keys in our van and was very concerned about what to do. Thankfully, Richard was able to use a coat hanger and retrieve the keys. On Wednesday, the kids and I picked Dick up in downtown Los Angeles and then headed to Universal Studios; it was another beautiful, clear, warm day. We had a wonderful time there with lots to see. Richard prepared us a huge, delicious chicken and spaghetti supper. Then at about 8 p.m. Darlene and I left to go bowling. Our bed felt good again after not getting home until about 11:10 p.m.

The next day, we took off as soon as we all could get ready, and we went to some nice areas and parks along the ocean. The waves were so big and pretty; we walked out on a short pier to where some people were fishing. Later, Dick was trying to get a picture of Alicia and rather neglectfully waited too long, and a wave knocked her down and she got soaking wet. The other girls had wet pants and shoes also by the time they finished playing.

In the evening, Richard and Darlene and Dick and I watched two shows of Joker's Wild being filmed; Amy stayed home with the girls. [A couple years later when we were visiting in California again, Dick and I stood in line to see the Bob Newhart show. We were in line for over two hours! The guard said no show is worth standing in the rain all that time. At least we had umbrellas- - -many did not. I thought it was really worth it, and it was exciting to see Bob Newhart in person.] After watching Joker's Wild, Richard and Darlene took us to a Cuban restaurant for supper, where we had a very good meal! We called Amy first to make sure she was handling the four girls all right which she said she was. So we got home between 8:30 and 9:00 p.m.

Friday, we got off as soon as we could to go to Knott's Berry Farm. Amy could come with us because she had the day off from school for Washington's birthday. Knott's Berry Farm had free admission for kids ages three to eleven that day so we decided to go. It was extremely crowded because of all the school children there, but we still were able to go on many of the rides and had lots of fun. In the evening, Dick and I went to a mall and browsed around awhile and had our supper. When we came back to the apartment, Darlene and Amy had all the girls to bed and sleeping which was a nice treat for me. Dick always kept us busy and hopping on our trips and vacations; he wanted to pack in as much as he possibly could and see all we could see, which we sure did! When we returned home, I used to say that I needed a vacation after our vacation trip.

On Saturday we were on our way to San Diego by 7 a.m. Darlene and Amy went with us also. We met the missionary serving the Christian Reformed Church at 10 a.m. for a tour of his work in one of the very poor villages near the border. So our girls had their first seven hours in northwestern Mexico in Tijuana, Baja California. There was no plumbing in this village, and they had just gotten electricity three months ago. At the missionary's home, we had a nice lunch of pan, pop, relishes, and pie. The kids thought it was neat when we were seated at a huge round table with a turntable in the middle that went around with the food on it.

The girls got a kick out of the donkeys in Mexico that were painted to look like zebras. We shopped briefly at a nice market, and the kids bought some souvenirs. We found a really nice motel back across the border. We fell to bed exhausted a bit after 10 p.m.

Sunday we went to church where a friend's brother was one of the pastors. We ate lunch at McDonald's, and then went to the zoo. We spent a good four hours there; San Diego Zoo is one of the largest in the world with over 3,700 animals and 660 different species. It is so huge, 100 acres in size, pretty, and clean---really nice! It has been awarded one of the best zoos in the world. We ate supper and then were back to Darlene's apartment by 8:45 p.m.

Monday was my laundry day again, and then Richard took us fishing for about four hours in the ocean off the Redondo Beach Pier. Kristi was the only one who caught any: a nice big fish called a California Corbina. The girls were pretty excited about it. Then Darlene and I went home and finished the laundry and let the two little ones nap.

That afternoon Dick went back to the beach with the two older girls and let them take their shoes and socks off and play on the beach for a couple hours. After laundry, I started packing up. Richard fixed Kristi's fish along with some other ones---a fantastic meal! Darlene contributed some delicious chocolate fudge that she had made. Later, Richard and Dick still went and bought us some sundaes and malts. The kids have really enjoyed a few days of being able to wear shorts.

We were up at 5:30 a.m. and on our way by 7:00 a.m. which is not too bad for having to get all the kids fed and dressed. We really had a nice stay at Richard, Darlene, and Amy's apartment, but it was exciting to be on our way once again. As we are riding along, I am thinking how beautiful California is . . . more so than I even remembered from when I lived there. No wonder so many people move and settle there. It is really a clean area with lots of pretty landscaping and very neat looking along the roads and expressways. But there is the problem with the bad smog in the summertime; we were there at wintertime, the best time.

Las Vegas was our next stop, and we had our lunch there at a huge place called Circus Circus. It had the largest and best organized buffet luncheon we ever had. It was $2.50 a plate, all you could eat plus drinks and desserts! We let the kids try the nickel slot machines. Boy, were they surprised when 20 nickels came back after only a couple tries, and they were allowed to scoop them all up and put them in their pockets. While we were letting them try the machines, a lady pointed out the sign that anyone under 21 had to stay out of the game area- - -whoops! Then we were on our way again. We drove through some pretty scenery with huge rocks and beautiful red colors, made especially pretty with the sun setting and highlighting the bright, vivid colors! We had a disaster when we stopped to eat supper. Alicia spilled water two times, Kristi had two spills, and then even I spilled my pop, so a total of five spills at one meal! Needless to say, the waitress looked pretty disgusted as we left. We drove on for a couple more hours and stayed in Nephi, Utah. Unfortunately, the motel was a bit dirty, the toilet made a noise all night, and the heater was so loud that I finally shut it off so I could fall asleep. Then the semis were so loud since we were right on the main road. I also heard a baby crying in the night; therefore, I did not get much sleep, but the others did okay.

We ate breakfast in Utah, then we were on the way to Salt Lake City. We saw the great tabernacle in the distance, saw a sign about Osmonds Studios, and drove past Salt Lake. We had our lunch in Idaho. The rest of the day was spent driving through probably the most beautiful part of our whole trip---mountains full of snow! We drove along Bear Lake which is a huge lake tucked in a valley. We went over three passes and were mostly on dry roads. However, my two-hour driving shift was first on ice and slush, and then more snow covered roads. Yet the beauty was unsurpassed! We arrived in Jackson, Wyoming by 4 p.m., but the Grand Tetons were once again covered with clouds, and I again did not even get a glimpse of them. I am beginning to wonder if there is such a thing as the Grand Tetons [as I missed seeing them on other trips too]. It looked like more snow coming to Jackson, so we decided to keep going and reach the other side of the mountains. Dick drove two and a half more hours to Riverton, Wyoming, where we had the most delicious pizza at Pizza Hut. Pretty good . . . we ate in a different state for each meal today! Then we stayed at a super nice Best Western for the night.

We were on the road by 7:30 a.m., a nice, early start. Our winter coats had to be hauled out once again. I really enjoyed my breakfast this morning, a nice danish and a chocolate malt! I drove my two hours which brought us to Casper, Wyoming. When Dick drove there was very little snow, but he kept hitting spots on the road that were wet and sloppy. We saw a small herd of deer. We came to the outskirts of the Blackhills at 12:30 p.m. We drove through all the prairie dog areas, we saw some buffalo, and a few deer. Then Dick wanted to take the Needles highway, but the sign said the road was closed in three miles. Well, we went on it anyway, and after the three miles we came to a sign . . . "Travel at your own risk; road not serviced in winter." Now to my thinking, that means it would be best to turn around! Dick, however, decided to keep going a few more miles along winding curves. Then we came to a point where the road was blocked, and said "closed" after we came all that way! Dick said if it did not look any worse than what we had traveled on, then we should go on. So we went past the barricade, and it was not long until it was MUCH worse, but by then it was almost too late to turn around. I crept along very cautiously, driving a lot of time in the lowest gear. I sure did not want to slide off the side of the mountain! In places, I wondered how we would make it up the steep grade with the snow; I was very concerned but kept pushing on. The Needles rock was pretty, but needless to say, I was so relieved when we got on the main road again. I wondered quite a few times if we were going to make it out again. [Of course, there were no cell phones then, and how would we have been able to get help when we were in the middle of nowhere on a closed road! I was afraid we would get stuck and have to stay there until spring! That was a scary experience for me, and my husband now admits that it probably was not the best thing to do!]

We saw beautiful Mount Rushmore again. It is unbelievable and so amazing to see those huge heads carved in granite 400 feet above where you stand. The faces are 60 feet from top to bottom, each eye is about 11 feet across, and the noses are 20 feet long. It took 14 years altogether to complete it because of the weather and fundraising. We went on and stayed at a Best Western in Rapid City for the night; it was really nice and very clean. All the girls were sleeping by 8:30 p.m.

Friday, and we were on our way again by 7:15 a.m. We stopped at famous Wall Drug in South Dakota, and the kids all chose a souvenir. A lot of shops were closed because it was off season. Dick bought some of the very delicious, freshly baked doughnuts there, and we had some apple juice in the car to go with them- - -a real nice mid-morning snack. There is not much to write today, as we have been traveling and traveling over the rolling, brown, treeless plains. We talked about how beautiful we think Michigan is compared to this, but to the people on the plains and wide open spaces, it is probably pretty. They may enjoy being able to see for miles and miles in all directions. We crossed into North Dakota about 3:30 p.m. and arrived at the Kuipers' home (our cousins) late afternoon, where we stayed for a couple nights.

We relaxed and visited on Saturday. The girls had a day to just enjoy playing all day with different toys. The Kuipers family fixed us grilled venison steaks for dinner which were very tasty. We looked at some slides that we had along and viewed some of their slides in the evening. I had a new experience there which was sleeping on a water bed. The first night I did not sleep very well at all . . . every time Dick turned over I felt like I was in a storm at sea! The second night I slept better but probably only because I was so exhausted I could have slept anywhere.

My cousin Betty fixed bacon and eggs, and we left their home at 9 a.m. There were a few inches of snow on the road as we left, but it has not slowed us down much. Regarding our road trip, some said we should have flown, because we could do it as cheap as driving. I have not regretted our decision at all. We have seen so much beauty and unusual scenery, and the kids did well. There were some trying moments, but I have them at home during my regular days also. They played very well most of the time and had plenty to keep them occupied over those many, many miles.

We crossed into Minnesota about noon, and traveled through the rolling farmland all afternoon. We had our lunch, and then I helped with homework for about two hours straight. We always had good cooperation with their teachers, and they would send along homework, so that they would not get behind in school when on a trip. The teachers always felt what they experienced and saw on the trips could never be taught in a classroom. There was some snow in Minnesota and Wisconsin, but the roads were dry. We ate supper at 7:30 p.m. in Black Hills Falls in Wisconsin. Then I put the kids to bed in the back of the car by 8:30 p.m. I also managed to get a little sleep before driving my shift from 11 p.m. until 1:00 a.m. Dick took over driving north of Chicago; he drove for three hours and made good time, getting us all the way to Muskegon. It was a total of 1,030 miles from cousin Carl's in North Dakota to our doorstep. We arrived home at quarter to 6:00 a.m. We quickly put everyone into their cold beds while the house was warming up, and we slept until about 9 a.m. Then we called my folks and went out there for breakfast. When we drove in they surprised us and had a "Welcome Home" sign hanging outside above the garage door.

The girls got right back into the swing of things and the older two went over to their friend's house for the afternoon. Nichole, Alicia, and I all had good afternoon naps. Looking back, it seems like we were in a different world for three weeks; it almost seems like a dream. The Lord sure was good to us as we traveled through all of those states and went many miles making that first family trip in 1983 a well remembered one! The total mileage for the trip was 6950 miles! It was great to go, but it felt good to return home also. It left me with a wonderful, new appreciation for our home and a new zeal and enthusiasm for my work and duties. I guess that is what vacations are supposed to do and why we take them.

To sum up the trip, God was in control of our travels and our family, and it was so wonderful to enjoy God's beauty in nature. It was good having all that family time, and visiting with sister, brother-in-law, niece, and cousins. It was fun showing our children new things, hearing their laughter and delight. They witnessed many wonderful sights on this trip---majestic mountains, the Grand Canyon, the ocean waves, the stately palm trees, the giant rocks, Mount Rushmore, the flat plains, the orange orchards, and lakes and waterfalls.

They were fairly young on that trip, but some of the girls still remember parts of it. As I mentioned before, we did a lot of traveling over the years. Thus, the children soon enjoyed traveling and do it now in their married years as much as they can. Talking about the beauties of nature on our long trip, I will include an excerpt from a devotional I wrote:

> Psalm 19:1-2, "The heavens declare the glory of God; the skies proclaim the work of His hands. Day after day they pour forth speech; night after night they display knowledge." We have had very little snow thus far this winter, and yesterday I took a picture of our green yard yet on January 16. Then this afternoon things changed, and it started snowing HUGE flakes. I do not know if

I ever saw them so big . . . some maybe two and a half inches long! Mid-afternoon I wanted to go to our local post office, so I bundled up for a walk. It was so very beautiful! I thought of the phrase "take time to smell the roses." That was what I was doing, only enjoying God's beautiful snowflakes and the awesome splendor with the snow clinging to bushes and trees. If we only take time and look, we can witness Him in so many things! We need to take this attitude more in the coming year and "Be still and know that He is God." Also, I have been reading a lot of books of late about the Amish, and that is their feeling also. Do not have your life so filled with material things and "clutter" that you cannot see God. Have this be your prayer today and ask yourself these questions: 1. What is cluttering up my life so I cannot easily see and hear God? 2. Am I taking the time in the hustle and bustle of life to see the BIG SNOWFLAKES, witnessing God's creation and His love for us? His handiwork is everywhere- - -in the storms, in the birds that sing, in the flowers that bloom, flying butterflies, in the big snowflakes, and He is even in our hearts if we are open to Him!

Do we take time to notice and enjoy God's handiwork? Spring and fall are my favorites, but winter has so many breathtaking scenes also. I never tire of the beautiful pine trees laden with snow, or of the trees stripped bare of leaves but covered with myriads of shapes and forms made of snow. How special it is to see the streams and rivers half frozen, dotted with rocks and logs covered with snow; ice and snow clinging to tree branches and bushes making an enchanting winter wonderland; icicles glistening in the moon light, a field of pure white snow without a mark or track to mar the beauty. What fascinating beauty if we dare stop long enough to see it! I can still picture in my mind the four beautiful swans I saw this afternoon flying gracefully with the blue contrasting sky in the background. When we take time to witness such handiwork, all we can do is stand back with awe and praise the Creator of such splendor. Psalm 8:9, "O Lord, our Lord, how majestic is Your Name in all the earth!" Are you standing back and looking?

FAMILY ACTIVITIES, BATS, SCARES

> "Search me, O God, and know my heart: try me, and know my thoughts: and see if there be any wicked way in me, and lead me in the way everlasting" (Psalm 139:23-24 KJV).

The years continued to fly by with us meeting new challenges and doing new things. No more baby years with all the diapers to be changed, but then years of more chasing around as the girls became involved in more at school, with their friends, at church, and in sports. A new chapter too in my life, since in 1986 all four of the girls were in school (although Alicia was there only three full days for kindergarten). It took me almost four months to adjust to the idea of having all four in school including my "baby." She had been my little pal and went with me everywhere when her three siblings were in school. It was hard for me when I realized that the baby and toddler stages were forever gone . . . harder when I realized how fast our four girls were growing up!

We did various family activities that were special to the girls as they were growing up. Those were the years to show them new and interesting things. Dick would take them to the country to hunt for caterpillars and show them what plants to find them on. He had a couple of old homemade wooden cages where they could place them, feed them, watch them make their cocoons, and learn patience while waiting for them to hatch. We hatched a lot of monarch butterflies over the years, and something Nichole still does every year.

Dick was the manager at the Oceana Canning Company in Shelby, three and a half miles away. This was a family-owned business, and they processed by canning, locally grown fruits and vegetables. During the summer it employed around 250 people (seasonal help) with multiple shifts, and 150 people worked during the wintertime. Later, it became Oceana Foods. Some evenings Dick would have some work to catch up on in his office, so he would take the girls with him (when they were not operating the second shift). They would bring their roller skates and skate all around the canning equipment on the hard cement floors. They could explore dark hallways and have a lot of fun playing hide and seek while Daddy was doing his work. A couple times for Christmas we had the unique experience of opening cans with Christmas presents inside. Dick and the girls took them to the canning factory and canned the presents. Another game the girls had fun with: Dick told them if they would put a little Fisher Price toy person in his lunch box in the morning, it would remind him to bring them a candy bar when he came home from work (from the snack machine). They did not overuse this little game.

Saturday mornings were special. Dick would take turns bringing each of the girls separately to a restaurant for breakfast. Dick also introduced the kids to the "creek walk" in New Era.

There is a creek half a block from our house, and they would hike alongside it for quite a ways. When we had our two dogs, they would go along and run to and fro. The girls could jump the creek at the narrowest places; they always thought the creek walk was so much fun. Sometimes they would walk down the railroad tracks that were no longer used (the train still used to come through a few times a week when the kids were real little). The tracks were torn out in 1982, and sometimes they would watch a crew taking up the tracks. The kids would have fun looking for the large spikes that were left behind. We have some of those souvenirs of that era in the attic. We felt a bit sad when trains no longer ran through New Era. However, a good thing came out of this when the old train track bed was made into a rail trail. The first eleven miles of the trail were completed from New Era to Hart in 1989, and it was the first rail trail with a paved surface in Michigan. The second half of the trail from New Era to Montague was paved in 1991, making the whole trail 22 miles in length. This trail can be seen from our kitchen window and was well used by the Walhout family. We did a lot of biking as a family---to Shelby for ice cream, to Shelby for freshly baked doughnuts at the bakery, to Montague for doughnuts, and just rides for the fun of it (my little four-year-old grandson calls it going on "bike hikes"). This trail is said to be one of Michigan's greatest rural rail trails. Riding along you can see corn and wheat fields, asparagus fields, hay crops, creeks, bridges, forests, cows, and apple and cherry orchards. The trail was extended a few years ago to connect to the Musketawa Trail (26 miles in length), so you can start in Hart and go all the way to Lake Michigan by Muskegon. Dick and I still ride bikes on it and when grandchildren are visiting, they ride with us. And something amazing . . . my older brother, Don, now 88 years old in 2022, rides 40 miles on the rail trail most days when weather permits. He says if he bikes less than 40 miles, it hardly feels like he has been out riding. I remember him saying once that his highest amount of miles in one year was 7000 miles---that is some record! That is way more miles than what we put on snowmobiling in the winters!

A fun day that the girls eagerly looked forward to was when our town of New Era held what was called Dutch Days. They had an ox roast (a pig) and a bountiful, free meal at the feed mill. The main downtown street was closed, and there were various vendors with their wares. Children looked forward to the many kids' games, pony rides, and the fun wooden shoe race (shoes provided) for different age groups. Sometimes a music group would sing, there was a watermelon eating contest, and water fights between the firemen. The biggest event of the day was when a plane would fly over and drop coupons (my brother-in-law, Rich, was often the pilot). The coupons were for items that people could get for free at the local stores downtown and other nearby businesses. Our girls sure found their share of coupons, since a lot of the coupons came floating right by our house or even in the woods behind us. After many years, Dutch Days was discontinued and a smaller New Era festival took its place.

Dick also thought of something that made Christmastime special for the girls. He told them they could sleep under the Christmas tree on Christmas eve. So they would sleep in their sleeping bags along with a number of their favorite stuffed animals. Dick would always join them for a while and tell them some of his made-up stories. They always looked forward to this year after year. And a tradition that was passed down from Dick's family was for the kids to lay their clothes out the night before (the clothes that they were going to wear on Christmas day). During the night, Santa came and hid the clothes with little presents in them. They always had to leave some milk and a few cookies for Santa on a plate, and the cookies always disappeared during the night (except for a couple of bites). They were always so excited and anxious to begin early looking for their clothes, that we had to set a limit on how early they could begin hunting for them on Christmas morning. This was another unique, fun tradition!

A funny thing happened when the kids were 1, 3, 5, and 7 years old. I let the three older girls stay by the fountain in the Muskegon Mall for five minutes while I went to a store (I could see them and keep an eye on them). When I came back they were so happy about the pennies and nickels they fished out of the water. It never crossed my mind that they might do that, nor did they think that it might be wrong to take them out. It was nothing too serious, but I did make them put the money back in the water.

Sunday night popcorn was another thing Dick started doing with the girls. He would sit the little ones up on the kitchen counter to help. A couple of the girls keep up the tradition and still have popcorn on Sunday nights. It is great for families to have their own special traditions.

When we were married, Dick owned a '35 Plymouth that became nicknamed the "Putt Putt." Many times our girls and others rode around the countryside with Dick in the old Putt Putt. They would have so much fun with this---often sitting on Daddy's lap to help steer and when older, learning to drive it with the stick shift.

We did things together as a family like learning to play tennis. We had older wooden rackets, but they still worked, and in the evenings we would go up to one of the two courts in town and play three on three. Canoeing was another fun thing as a family, and we did it many times on the White River (about 12 miles away). The girls, however, were jumpy about spiders and worried that spiders would land on them or fall in the canoe if they went too close to overhanging branches. There were a couple of extra tip-overs because of this fear of spiders.

Dick had an idea to give the girls an opportunity to experience something new. He decided to purchase four baby ducks, a dozen chickens, and a goose from our local feed mill to raise. We made a large pen for them on the floor in our garage. It was the girls' responsibility to feed them, water them, and change the newspapers we had on the floor. Once the fowl grew too big to keep in the garage, they were brought out to Grandma and Grandpa Walhout's farm. They had an old chicken coop on their place and a tank that could be filled with water for the ducks. Finally, they were big enough to be butchered and someone in the neighborhood did the deed for us. We still had to cut the birds up and wrap them in order to store them in the freezer.

This was the spring we added two more members to our family. First, Dick allowed Kristi to buy her own puppy for one dollar from friends. Not too long after that puppy, we got another one. Dick had always wanted a Dalmatian, and he thought it would be more fun for the pups to have company. We had a good place for them . . . in the fenced in backyard that had been the kids' play area when they were little. So Dick and the girls made a dog coop inside of the garage from which the dogs could go in and out as they pleased into the backyard. We made the decision that this would be a good time for the girls to have the dogs, since a couple of them were really afraid of dogs! Talking it over, we had thought the best way for them to get over that fear was to have puppies so the girls could get used to them from little up. It worked and cured them of that fear. Later on, they used to tease me and say I needed some baby bats to raise to get rid of my fear. I admit, I have discovered I have a gigantic fear of bats, my phobia for sure! Before we had the eaves of this older home boxed in, we frequently had bats as visitors, much to my dismay and horror.

Speaking of bats . . . these furry little beasts with sharp, pointed teeth, I have some intriguing bat stories that happened in our house. One time I was vacuuming under something in the attic and caught a bat on the end of the vacuum hose. The suction held it there, and it was screeching away. I panicked, left the vacuum running, and ran downstairs. My husband could not be bothered at work that day, so I called a neighbor a few houses down from us. He was my "knight in shining armor" that day and helped a lady in distress (me!). He caught it and took care of it, which I was very thankful for! Another time, Dick had taken the girls to the Hart Fair for the evening. I had just sat down in my recliner to enjoy a nice chocolate shake while watching some TV. All of a sudden, a bat came circling around in the living room. I jumped up, spilled my shake, and ran into the front room and closed the sliding pocket door. There I sat with nothing to do until the family came home and Dick took care of the unwanted bat. I had been much too frightened to go out in the living room by the bat!

A different time, a bat appeared upstairs where all the girls were sleeping. Dick was gone that night to a seminar for his work. When Nichole came downstairs, woke me up, and told me that either a bird or a moth was flying around upstairs, I was pretty sure I knew exactly what it more than likely was! Since Dick was gone, I was the one who had to be brave and check it out. I was filled with dread and great fright as I climbed cautiously up the stairs. Sure enough, a bat flew right by me in the hallway, skimming my shoulder, filling me with fear and trepidation! Two of the girls and I ran into a bedroom where another daughter was sleeping (and there was probably some squealing as we ran). Kristi woke up and asked what were we all doing in her bedroom?! We quickly vacated that room and somehow the bat wound up in there, and we swiftly shut the door. I grabbed a sleeping bag and stuffed it along the bottom of the door hoping the bat could not escape. I proceeded to route all four of the girls downstairs to sleep for the rest of the night, and closed the stair door. In the morning, I called another friend, two houses from us, and he came and captured the bat. He carefully removed the sleeping bag and actually found the bat on the bag.

Dick has had to capture a bat on some occasions in the middle of the night- - -chasing it around in his underwear and with a tennis racket (and me safely hiding under the covers in bed). Dick has also been awakened several times with a phone call in the middle of the night by a lady who is a distant relative. She and her mother were plagued with bats in their older home, and she also had a great fear of them. She knew she could call on Dick for help. My greatest fear when Dick spends the night away and I have to stay alone is that a bat will appear. Mice, I can take . . . I just cannot deal with "mice" that fly! Then while our daughter and family were visiting last year, one appeared in the bedroom where two of the young boys were sleeping. It did not bother them in the least---they thought it was the neatest thing lying there watching it fly around, and they were not scared at all. Finally, one boy went and woke up Ryan (their dad). Ryan remembered seeing a plastic bag hanging in the back by the basement steps, so he knew where to find leather gloves and a tennis racket. He took care of the bat, and when we woke up in the morning, we heard the story about the bat in the bedroom. At first, I thought the boys made up the story to tease me knowing of my phobia, but I found out it was true. Anyway, maybe with extra company going in and out doors, a bat had sneaked in unnoticed. Thankfully, we very seldom have a bat in the house anymore, and enough "batty" stories. As a precaution though, I have a couple devices in the attic and a couple in the basement that continually transmit a sound that bats are not supposed to like. I do not know if they work, but it makes me feel better having them there! I keep the phone and phone numbers right by my bed in case I need to call for help if a bat appears when my husband occasionally stays overnight at a tractor show or some other event.

Next, a few more special things we did with our children. One thing I liked to do when the girls were younger was give each one their own plot of ground in my big garden. I would mark off their sections with stakes and strings. They could plant whatever vegetables and flowers they wanted. It was their responsibility to weed, water, and harvest what they had grown. They all like to garden or plant flowers now around their own homes.

In the summer we liked doing special things during the different days of the week. I read about this in a magazine, so I implemented it into our summers. There would be a friend's day when they invited someone over, a bake day when that person helped bake something, a special day when we would go to a park, have a picnic, or go swimming. One day of the week we made a different lunch and filled up a six-cup muffin tin for each child. You had six places then to put a sandwich, fruit, chips, cookies, crackers, marshmallows, or chocolate chips to list a few of the choices. The kids really thought that was neat and called it their surprise lunch.

Roller skating is something we did quite often as a family, and the girls learned how to skate at a young age (sometimes they had skates on at two years old already). The boys' group from our church often had a night when they would use the skating rink, and Dick would pick up a load of boys to take to the skate night. The girls and I would go along for these events, and it was a fun thing to do as a family. Sometimes we picked up so many kids that Dick would drive our van, and I would take our car.

A really special thing for the girls was when they were able to experience their first plane rides in a big jet. We were able to get free tickets for them by entering the "Kids Fly Free" promotion through Ralston Cereals, and a special deal through Piedmont Airlines. We had to send in eight cereal box tops for each child and one dollar and fifty cents processing, and then we received the tickets. The only stipulation was there had to be an adult along with each child, so Grandpa and Grandma Walhout were invited along too. They had never been to California so jumped at the chance. We spent three days in San Francisco and stayed at a motel right near the ocean and not far from Seal Rock. Then we took the Amtrak train to Los Angeles. It was an eleven hour ride through many tunnels, over lots of bridges, and along the ocean. We could walk around in the train or sit and enjoy all the pretty scenery. The remaining ten days were spent in Santa Monica with my sister, husband, and daughter. We took in a lot of the sights around there. It was quite an experience planning, grocery shopping, and fixing meals for eleven people, but everyone pitched in and helped so it went okay. We were busy and saw a lot---Universal Studios, Disneyland, Knott's Berry Farm, Huntington Library, and La Brea Tar Pits. It was an exceptionally nice trip, and we were thankful it all went well and that we had more wonderful memories to tuck away.

When the girls were in junior high and high school, we put up a basketball hoop. It was a very worthwhile investment as the kids practiced shooting baskets a good deal, and this probably helped them when they were on the girls' basketball teams in high school. Two of the girls played basketball and both were starters on their team. The girls and I played a considerable amount of basketball over the years, and they had four cousins nearby that often joined us for special times of fun. All the girls were involved in sports in grade school as well as high school. Besides basketball, they were involved in volleyball, soccer, and softball. The Christian high school the girls attended was 30 miles away from New Era; so the high school years were very busy with trips for sports, practices, games, and also busy with choir, band, and school plays.

Whereas the grade school years were busy with homework, piano lessons, spelling bees, and science fairs . . . the high school years were busy with lots of homework, friends, sports, and extracurricular activities. I would consider it a treat when we all sat down together for our supper meal. Many days I would pack seven lunches; one for Dick, two for the two girls in grade school, and four for the two girls in high school when they would have to stay after school for a game and needed something for their supper. I would have to pack lunches the night before, since I had to get up early in the morning to drive my bus run. Thinking of all that busyness, I could never handle that sort of life now!

I think, though, I have filled you in on enough family activities and need to move on to more stories in keeping with my title and especially about "The Mighty Angels." I will reflect on how the Lord watched over us while raising our young girls, and how their *guardian angels* were right alongside them.

One day our daughters had two friends over to play after school when Kristi was six years old. They were playing nicely outside but all of a sudden, they brought Kristi in crying, and she was bleeding profusely! She had run through the open gate to the fenced-in area and caught her forehead on a sharp corner. It was a good thing she did not catch it any lower or the sharp point could have hit and harmed her eye. I kept debating whether to bring her to the doctor, since I got the bleeding stopped, but there was quite a gash. Finally, a couple of the younger girls and I walked Kristi down to the doctor as his office was in town, only a block away. They immediately put seven stitches in. Kristi was so very good about it! She did not even cry when he injected the gash four or five times to numb it. It hurt badly though, and her eyes filled with tears, but she still did not cry. Later, she was glad she could show everyone and tell about it for "show and tell" at school. She had another mishap when Dick was gone to Chicago for a seminar for three nights. The second night he was gone, Kristi ran out the front porch too fast and went through the bottom of the storm door window with her arms and hands. She had several cuts on her right hand but thankfully nothing too serious! But that was not it for Kristi; we said that year, 1985, went out with a BANG when she crashed a wooden rocking chair through a front room window on New Year's Eve. We were thankful again Kristi did not get hurt, and that she went through a side window and not through the large middle picture window. Nor did we have the freezing cold air come in as only the inside window was broken and not the outer storm window too. It was certainly unintentional; she just rocked too hard and the chair was too close to the window.

But alas, broken glass stories are not limited to children. Once when Dick and I were visiting our daughter and family in South Dakota, he made an embarrassing mistake. We had stopped to look around at a very large greenhouse because they had a big variety of plants and other interesting items. My daughter and I were walking a bit ahead of Dick and were just ready to enter the large glass doors of the greenhouse when the right side of the door broke and shattered into millions of pieces right before our eyes! We were so shocked and surprised as bits of glass came cascading down in front of us, like a waterfall. We wondered if we had bumped something or what to make that happen! But then Dick came walking up from behind and confessed he accidentally kicked a stone too hard and it hit the door! At least the inside panel was still intact. It was not a fun thing for him to have to walk up to the cashier and admit that he was responsible for the broken glass door! The cashier, thankfully, did not seem too concerned and said they had insurance for that sort of thing. We never forget that incident whenever we stop at that particular greenhouse (like we did recently when visiting our daughter again). The lesson learned- - -Dick said he had better stop kicking stones as he was in the habit of doing on walks.

Our third daughter, Nichole, at about five years, had a scary thing happen one day when I took the girls over to my sister's pool to swim. My sister and I were visiting next to the pool while the kids were playing nicely when all of a sudden my sister hollers---"Get Nichole!" Here she had been playing around in the shallow end which was about three feet deep. She was wearing an inflatable ring around her so she could float. Somehow, she had tipped completely over with her feet kicking up in the air, and the ring was holding her upside down! She could not right herself again! I grabbed her as quickly as I could, but she had swallowed several mouthfuls of water already. She cried and cried and finally we just went home. She was too scared and did not want to swim again that day, and it also scared me!

Nichole had another scary thing happen to her when she was almost 15 years old. Nichole is not bothered by heights, so she was always willing to climb around on the very high roof of our two-story home to clear off snow when we had large accumulations. Nichole and Alicia had been all over the roof pushing down the deep snow one winter day. They would sit on the peaks like riding a horse- - -Nichole even on the very highest ones! On this particular day, they were helping their dad get some snow off near the porch roof to make sure it would not start leaking. After finishing shoveling, she was coming down on the back side of the roof and she noticed a bunch of snow yet over a bedroom.

Nichole went up to knock it down from the highest part of the roof. She said it all happened so fast she did not even know what happened . . . whether she slid over to the roof's valley and then down, or right down the steepest part. Down she went and by her imprint in the snow, she came within one foot of the sidewalk---way too close for comfort! Her face went in the snow, and she was worried about losing her contacts, but she did not. Only our dog, Rocky, witnessed it, and he could not tell us how it happened. Thankfully, she fell in the large pile of snow they had shoveled off and not on the sidewalk! I did not even want to think what could have happened if she had landed on the sidewalk coming from that height! Now we hope she has a little more respect for heights!

One final adventure about Nichole happened when Alicia was 18 years old and Nichole was 20 years old. Dick and I had left them home alone and went to Gulf Shores for a week for a special get-together for my sister and husband's 50th wedding anniversary. This was also the new millennium, and we continued with heat, power, computers, and without any major crisis that people were so concerned about when that transition took place. We allowed the girls free use of the snowmobiles during the time we were gone, and we hoped they would not encounter any breakdowns. We started wondering about the state of things back home when we got an email saying, "We've had our share of excitement here, but don't worry, all is well." Which of course made me very concerned! Alicia wrote about this accident shortly after it happened, and this is what she wrote:

> As you heard Nichole say on the phone, she flipped your wonderful snowmobile, Dad. But she did not actually watch it happen. You have to think of poor, little

me who was sitting on the Jag snowmobile watching this whole awful scene pass before my eyes. What I vouch for was the snowmobile all of a sudden jumping into the air, Nichole falling off, and the machine doing a complete roll in the air. This really happened! It did not roll on the ground; this was all in the air! But the worst part was when it came back from its time to fly, it landed right on Nichole. That scared me and I jumped off my snowmobile, ran to her, and kept yelling if she was okay. But she just kept saying, "Oh, I'm so embarrassed!" I kept asking her if she was all right, and she just told me to shut off the machine. Then I saw her leg under the snowmobile, and I thought it could be broken and tried to lift the machine off of it. The second time of trying, I lifted it right up which was quite a feat in itself, and she was able to get her leg out. At least it was not broken. Anyway, that is my side of the story.

Nichole said she woke up the next morning very stiff, and her neck and her leg had a couple tiny bruises---other than that, she was okay. The reason she was so embarrassed is because this accident happened by the New Era Christain School soccer field in full view of her previous teacher and the junior high school kids. They watched the whole incident---even with binoculars. A cousin of the girls, who was in the classroom that day, said they had a ten minute break watching them. They all were wondering if Nichole would get up and if the snowmobile was okay. This all took place because she hit a patch of ice. So quite a thing to have happen, and we were not even home. I think Nichole's *guardian angel* protected her from great harm that day, and Alicia's *guardian angel* helped her pick up the back of that 550 pound machine high enough for Nichole to pull her leg out from underneath. And amazingly, there was no damage to the snowmobile either!

Another extraordinary story about Alicia occurred in the mountains. We had been on a family trip to Mexico when the children were older and came back through Colorado. We decided to go up the majestic mountain, Pikes Peak (14,000 feet). It is quite the experience going so high, driving around those many curves with no guard rails. It is fun and exciting, but scary too! As we neared the top, it started snowing; this was a big surprise in the middle of the summer. After winding around a great many more sharp corners, we finally arrived at the top. Later, some of our group was in the gift shop and others were wandering around outside, enjoying the view and the experience of snow, lightning, and thunder in the summertime. However, soon the staff was walking around and telling everyone to go inside because of the lightning. During this process, somehow, Alicia did not hear the warning and remained outside. A staff member went to her, and as he was telling her to go inside, he fell to the ground. He got up and said, "I think we were just struck by lightning!" Later, when she told us, she said she felt when she got zapped, like a lot of static electricity, and it made her feel funny. The whole time we rode back down the mountain and for the rest of the day, she felt a bit out of sorts and was tired. We figured the lightning went through the metal hair barrette she was wearing. She took it easy the rest of the day but was fine again the next day. She will never forget her frightening and "shocking" experience on top of Pikes Peak!

The girls were not the only ones to experience close calls and perhaps have *guardian angels* right alongside providing protection from great harm. One evening, I was alone heading to one of the girl's basketball games in Muskegon. I was almost there and had to get in the middle lane on Apple Avenue to make a left turn. I did everything appropriately when all of a sudden there were two headlights barreling down at me---coming fast, straight at me, also in the middle lane. It was way too close for comfort, and I was thinking I was in for a head-on collision for sure! Where did that car come from all of a sudden and why in the turn lane at that particular spot? I think we both swerved left (which was good!), and I was so very thankful I could proceed to the basketball game.

One more scary incident for me that I decidedly and very clearly remember is when I went to grab something from the cupboard in our back area. To get to our old basement, we have to descend down nine cement steps which make a turn at the bottom. On one side of the steps is the old stone foundation, and the other side is made of partly cement blocks and some stones. I have a cupboard behind the basement door and shelving along the ledge for storage. I often go back there to retrieve canned goods or to store something. To get to this back area, I must open the basement door, step over the raised door sill, and go down one step to a small landing. I do not know just how it happened, but I must have tripped going over the high door sill and fell face down, on my stomach, arms stretched ahead of me while I started sliding down the first few steps of the nine steps. I let out a very weak scream (no one was around at the time) and thought for sure I was going to keep sliding down those hard, unforgiving cement steps, and probably bang my head forcefully on the wall of blocks or hit the stone wall! Thankfully, I stopped and I wonder if a *mighty angel* might have stopped me and was with me that day. I believe in angels! Happily, I was okay except for a couple of scrapes. I could have lain there at the bottom with a broken neck or bleeding and unconscious until someone came home and found me. It was a very frightening and shocking thing for me for sure! I still get all shook up thinking about it, so now on to a funny story to change our thoughts.

When most of our girls were in their teens, Dick wound up having more free time in the evenings. In fact, he had more free time than he wanted so when the janitorial job became available at New Era Christian grade school (where our children attended), he applied and got the job. He was still working at Country Dairy full time too. Often, with a couple of our girls helping, he could complete the work before supper. One day, I tackled the big project of cleaning out our old basement, not a job I like doing at all! Dick came down to see how I was doing, and then told me he was leaving to work at the school for a while. I kept working away; later I had to go upstairs, and when I pulled on the door at the top of the basement steps, it was hooked. My husband had locked me in the basement! But it was an accident; he just hooked it automatically without thinking. Thankfully, I happened to have the phone down with me, and I could call him at school to come home and let me out! What a husband I have who locks his loving wife in the basement!

Recently something unusual happened to my husband which is a good story. He was driving his pickup truck to a parts store. It was a bit stuffy in the truck, so he rolled the window down. Almost right away, something flew in very quickly. He looked down on his shirt and there was a huge ol' bumble bee on him! That probably would have made many young ladies (maybe some men) land in a ditch or hit a tree. In those few seconds the bumble bee crawled right down into his shirt pocket! Dick was afraid it would get mad and sting him through his thin shirt. He tried to gently hold the shirt away from his skin and was able to make it the rest of the way into the parking lot at the parts store. He jumped out of the truck as fast as he could (forgetting to release his seat belt which complicated things), and carefully unbuttoned his shirt and ripped it off. He shook it until the bumble bee flew away. That sneaky bee could have crawled down under his shirt which would have been worse yet! He asked me what a lady would have done . . . I said probably the same thing you did. No one wants to get stung by an angry bumble bee!

One more funny but scary story yet. This happened, again, when I was housecleaning but this time in our bedroom. I always start cleaning in a certain spot and work around the room. I was up to my desk which had a bunch of books on it. I took the whole stack and set them upright on a chair. My intention was to use the hose of the vacuum with the small brush attachment to vacuum the dust off the top of the books. I was interrupted, though, with fixing supper and other things and did not get back to the vacuuming job. That was not a problem, I would work in the room some more the next day. To explain, this was an old canister-style vacuum with a metal pedal you stepped on to start the machine. My husband and I proceeded to go to bed that night---the vacuum and books off to one side and out of our way. Can you imagine our panic, fright, and trepidation when all of a sudden in the middle of the night the vacuum started running?! Our first thought was there was a burglar in our house! But as we fumbled around and turned the lights on and checked out the situation, we could see what had happened. With the books upright on the chair, one or two books had to have come open just a tiny bit and moved a little, and like a domino effect knocked a book down on the floor. That book hit the pedal on the vacuum just right, making it turn on. What a thing to have happen in the middle of the night and get our hearts racing! And my foremost suggestion to you is do not ever leave a plugged in vacuum in your bedroom at night!

Thinking through these family times, some scary moments and close calls, it is very comforting to know God sends His *angels* to watch over us; they are right there alongside us every day. We will never know how many accidents or mishaps did not occur because God's *mighty angels* shielded us or perhaps changed our direction. As we face life and its various situations, we will encounter smooth roads along with rough roads. Be thankful for the blessings each day that allow us to keep traveling along the smooth roads. And praise God when we see evidence of the Lord working in our lives. But when we have the frustrations, burdens, trials, heartaches, and challenges and the roads become rough, we need to remember the Bible passages with promises that God is there with us---He is our Rock, our Fortress, our Deliverer, and He arms us with strength (II Samuel 22:2-3). We need to stand firm so we can face and overcome the struggles and storms of this world. It is necessary to keep "pressing on" and make our faith stronger through worship, praise, Bible study, fellowship with other Christians, and prayer.

One of my poems, "Clouds of Life", speaks about the valleys we sometimes have to go through and the rough times we may need to face:

As we are traveling along, I'm enjoying the sky so bright.
The sky is filled with huge clouds so fluffy and white!
I'm thinking . . . what beauties God often puts on display
And if we'd pay more attention, we'd see beautiful things each day.
It is fun to watch as the clouds keep floating along;
They even look happy, like if able, they'd burst into song.
The beautiful clouds come big, small, and so very different in shape;
God is behind them, you see, deciding their fate.
So it is with us humans as along life's path we trod;
Our destiny---and our whole life is planned by God.
And we have our many "clouds in life" as we go daily down the road.
Some clouds are dark, gray, dreary bringing in the cold.
Other clouds might look scary, angry, filled with fear;
And the results of these clouds may be hurt and sadness when they hover near.
There are clouds of disappointment, heartaches, and despair;

But God is there amongst the clouds helping with what we must bear.
Our Great God can help make these dark, foreboding clouds cease.
He can readily turn the clouds back to white and filled with peace.
Hopefully the dark clouds will be there for only a little while---
Then the big white, fluffy clouds will come back bringing a smile.
I'm looking in the sky to see what clouds I find;
And thinking that it's God who orchestrates which "clouds of life" will be mine. (9/11/16.)

When there are clouds of disappointment, adversity, and despair or when we are faced with the storms in our lives, remember that Jesus calmed the storms and stilled the waves. This verse is remarkable in Psalm 107:29, "He stilled the storm to a WHISPER; the waves of the sea were HUSHED." Christ did this for His disciples during a storm, and He can do this for us today! We know the turbulence and unrest will come for God has never promised Christians a life of ease without the difficulties, trials, or storms. But He promises to be with us during the challenges and hard times of life. Isaiah 43:2 says, "When you pass through the waters [hardships], I will be with you; and when you pass through the rivers [difficulties], they will not sweep over you." Even through the darkest of nights we know that once again will dawn the glorious morning. And again . . . "In everyone's life some rain must fall." But we can look forward to the rainbows in our life since after the rains (struggles and tribulation) come the beautiful rainbows. Without the rains, we would miss out on the rainbows! "The rainbows of life come after the storms" giving us hope, peace, fervor, and great comfort!

PARENTS, EARLY JOBS, ENCOURAGEMENT

"I have told you all this so that you will have peace of heart and mind. Here on earth you will have many trials and sorrows; but cheer up, for I have overcome the world" (John 16:33 Liv. New Testament).

After relating experiences and stories concerning our four daughters, I will move on to us as parents. Dick had a few job changes over the years, but we were always able to keep living in New Era. He is still employed at Country Dairy, a mile and a half from our house where he has worked for over thirty years. At 75 years old, he now only works about ten hours a week for Country Dairy. Country Dairy has been a family owned business for four generations. The farm milks about 1,200 cows and processes their own milk, cheese, ice cream, and employs about 125 people. It bottles more than 70,000 gallons of milk per week. You can buy their products at the Farm Store on their premises and eat at their great restaurant.

As for me, for many years I very much enjoyed playing volleyball with a group of men and ladies one night a week but quit when I turned 70 years old. My jobs stayed pretty much the same over the years---bus driver, house cleaner, baker, cook, mender, advisor, nurse, chauffeur, laundry person, ironer, gardener, typist, consultant, mother, and wife. I am like my husband now and have shortened my workload and hours.

We look back and think of the many various chapters we have gone through in our married life. The chapter we faced when all the girls attended grade school, and then went on to high school. I think my hair started turning gray (just a little) when we had four teenagers at the same time, and then when they took driver's training, and we had to let these new drivers chauffeur us around. And a day of concern the first time they took the car "all alone" to their high school in Muskegon 30 miles away. They all managed this trial run okay, and I could relax as they became more experienced drivers. Then to college; and then graduating from college. Two of the daughters chose Dordt College in Sioux Center, Iowa and it was a hard chapter for me to face having them a 14 hour drive away. Maybe the most difficult chapter (for me anyway) is when the girls left "the nest" permanently and were married. I was happy and thrilled for them and the young men who became their life's partner, but all of a sudden they were gone from under our care and it was very different. So we had to face many different chapters and transitions. But thinking back over the years, the times and memories that stand out are the ones spent with my spouse and with my daughters, sons-in-law, grandchildren, and enjoying God's creation. We are very thankful that God has so richly blessed us!

My husband's interests include his three restored John Deere tractors and one Farmall. We enjoy taking tractor rides together (the Farmall has a nice wide seat for two), or sometimes each driving a tractor. We also join a group on Wednesday nights and cruise around the countryside in classic old cars; ours is a '66 Caprice. Dick enjoys going to tractor and car shows. His favorite is the Buckley Old Engine Show about two hours away, and he takes his restored tractors there to display them. It is a four day show in August, and it has a huge number of tractors and steam engines on exhibit. Also, Dick has his pilot's license and used to fly small planes and is very interested in aviation. Dick, some of our daughters, and guests they invite along attend the Oshkosh Airventure in Wisconsin every year at the end of July. This annual air show gathering of those interested in aviation is organized by the Experimental Aircraft Association and is the largest of any kind in the world! The show lasts a week and has more than 10,000 different aircraft on display. This is such a huge event with 642,000 people attending in 2019 which marked its 50th year. My husband, a daughter and husband, another son-in-law, and three grandsons attended the summer of 2021. One more of Dick's interests was his involvement in the jail ministry on Monday nights for many years. He counseled those who requested it in their jail cells. He enjoyed talking with the men on a one-on-one basis, and it was a chance to share his faith with them.

 I enjoy having a vegetable garden and landscaping our yard. One year I tackled the monstrous project of making a waterfall in our backyard. The hill of sand was there from adding on to our garage. Making the waterfall was a lot of work---I cemented it all together rock by rock! We also made a little creek from the base of the waterfall to a small pond where Dick keeps goldfish. Often frogs come to live by the pond, and it is fun seeing them sitting on the lily pads. The waterfall and creek really turned out nice, and people can see it as they go past our house. Next, Dick helped me make a small patio where we can sit and enjoy the waterfall. Another thing I did a couple summers ago was make a large gnome house in our backyard. We had a tree cut down on our property line, and I told the tree company workers to leave a ten foot stump. I decided I needed to do something creative with it, and with the help of a daughter's suggestion, came up with the idea of the gnome house. I have had lots of compliments on it. In fact, several people have stopped to take pictures, and a few more gnome houses have sprung up in Oceana County. I needed a son-in-law to help with the roof, since I did not know how to accomplish putting together and installing one. The gnome house is large enough that people can see it from downtown New Era and as they go up the hill on Garfield Road. Another interest for me is watching professional tennis, and I became an avid fan. A daughter went with me to Cincinnati, Ohio's tournament twice, and the first time we were able to see the top four players (at that time) in the world play. I even managed to get the top three autographs . . . including Roger Federer and Rafael Nadal, my favorites. Plus, Mr. Federer even used my black marker to sign some other autographs, and I asked him to return my marker and have kept it as a souvenir.

Usually my backyard looks nice with the gnome house, flowers, shrubs, many hostas, bark covered paths that little grandkids like to follow, a rock garden, wind chimes, and little critter ornaments hiding here and there. One time, however, when we returned home from a trip to Pennsylvania in June of 2015, we had a disaster! We came home to several inches of sand in the driveways, behind the garage, along the sides of the garage, in flower beds, in the lawn, in our basement, and down the streets of New Era. Dick's sister, who had been keeping an eye on the house while we were gone, called us and told us what had happened. But we never dreamed how extensive and deep the sand would be! There had been four inches of hard, steady rain which had washed a newly excavated hill behind us down through the woods and down the road. It took days and days and weeks to get it all cleaned up again. All that bending, shoveling, raking, lifting, and wheelbarrowing was very hard on this then-70-year-old lady. I did most of this very difficult task, since Dick was at work every day. The person who owned the property took the sand away for us. It took him ten trips with a tractor and a huge scoop. Each scoop could hold probably three wheelbarrows full of sand! We did not want that to ever happen again! When shoveling up some of the sand, we filled some sand bags and laid them along the back of our fence as a preventative measure. The owner also had the property seeded, straw put over it, and a plastic barrier put in around the edges. So it has never happened again, nor have we had four inches of steady rain again either!

After talking about that accumulation of unwanted sand, I will switch to talking about snow. I have mentioned previously about our interest in snowmobiling. I thoroughly savor and relish going out in the crisp fresh air, derive pleasure in driving a snowmobile, and delight in all the beauty as we ride along. Dick enjoys the sport also but more so when he can take young boys along who do not have the opportunity to snowmobile. He likes to give people their first taste of snowmobiling and the experience of learning to drive one. I related in an earlier chapter some close calls and mishaps that happened on our snowmobile rides when taking others along. But I did not mention a couple of accidents that Dick and I also experienced. We have snowmobiled a great number of miles over many years and feel we are experienced drivers. We always try to be careful and cautious, as they are powerful machines and people can get seriously hurt riding on them. Dick had a mishap a few years back that caused him much discomfort for several months. I was following behind him on my machine, and he tried to get up on a hard, crusty bank of snow along the road. When a snowbank is quite high, it is best to come at it straight which did not work out for him to do. He started up part of the bank at an angle, but he did not make it, and the big snowmobile tipped over and landed on top of Dick with him underneath lying on the bare, hard pavement. I thought, "Oh, no . . . a broken leg or arm." He wiggled himself out from under, and we tipped it right side up. The windshield had one corner broken out, some black trim came off, and the whole throttle mechanism was smashed and broke. He was able to get it started after a few tries, and we rode the rest of the way home on bare pavement. At least Dick did not have a broken leg or arm, but it turned out he had broken ribs, and it was very painful for him for a long time!

I had a similar thing happen on the way home from a snowmobile ride. We had been riding with four other young boys, and I went home a bit early to start our supper. I tried getting up a bank just across the road from our house on Garfield Road, but again I had to try at an angle. It was hard to hit it straight on since the roads were bare that day. I made it up on the bank of snow but somehow the snowmobile stayed right on the ridge of the snowbank, and I lost my balance and fell down three feet to the road. I hit the road with my body and looked up only to see my snowmobile coming down on top of me! I was embarrassed since a semi was up the road a little ways waiting to cross Oceana Drive, and the driver saw it happen when looking in her side mirror. An older gentleman coming from the east on Garfield Road also witnessed it. The lady semi-driver and the man came to see if I was okay. I told them I was. I had managed to get out from under the snowmobile which was lying on its right side, or maybe it was upside down; I'm not sure. I shut it off as it was still running. The three of us had to work hard to get the snowmobile righted again. The lady kept asking over and over if I was okay. After a couple of tries, I started the machine again and drove it on the bare road the rest of the way home. The snowmobile was okay except the handle bar was smashed down in the middle, but it could be popped back out. The windshield, though, was cracked in a couple places with a piece broken out of it; it had to be replaced. Me . . . well, I had a very poor night of sleep as I was sore in a lot of places! The right side of my neck was sore, my right arm and foot were sore, my back was sore, and I probably hit my head on the pavement but had my helmet on. It took a few days for my aches and pains to go away, especially my right leg which really hurt for a few weeks. I also must have hit something with the left side of my face in the accident, because it was a little swollen. My left cheek on my face has always been a tiny bit fuller since that day---a reminder to always be careful when riding a snowmobile! I recuperated from my accident and soon was on my trusty snowmobile once again.

Sometimes on an especially beautiful winter day, you can find me out in the fields alone on my bright red Ski Doo snowmobile, gliding and skimming across the snow in some orchards. I feel fairly safe going out alone when I can carry my phone along in case of an emergency. I did run out of gas once, but I could call Dick to bring some gas in a can, and I conveniently was right near a road. One time I had the misfortune of getting the machine stuck badly on a ridge between two fields (when I was by myself). Dick was at work, and I needed to get home within the hour to drive the school bus. What was I to do? I was not near any houses or close to a road. When I put it in reverse, it just went deeper in the snow. I tugged at it, tried lifting the back end around, but that is hard to do for one person in deep snow (my snowmobile would weigh about 470 pounds). I became so warm tugging and pulling and lifting; I finally took off my coat, scarf, helmet, and gloves. It took at least a half hour of hard work, but I finally was successful and happy that I could get home and still be on time for my afternoon bus run.

The kids were older at this point in our lives, so when I had to leave them to go on a trip with Dick, it was easier for me. And for many of our trips, the children were able to go along. Dick made a trip to Peru for a week as an advisor to an asparagus plant. We made three different trips to ski resorts near Denver, Colorado so the girls could ski, which they so enjoyed. Some other trips were to southern states, trips out east several times, and a trip with the girls to Washington, D.C. to see many of the important sights. Dick and I stayed at The Grand Hotel on Mackinac Island twice for very special occasions! We made quite a few trips to Tennessee and Gulf Shores to visit with my sister Eleanor and her husband, Rich, after they moved to Tennessee from New Era. Three of those times all the siblings and spouses met with

Rich and Elinor; they were such good family times of visiting, reminiscing, and having fun together. Dick and a daughter went to Indonesia when daughter Kristi, Jeff and family were there working for Wycliffe Bible Translators. Dick and I rode our Farmall tractor across the Mackinac Bridge two different years. They open the bridge up for tractors to cross around September 8, and it is a really interesting and fun experience to cross that long bridge with about 1,500 other tractors. Two of our daughters (and a cousin) always remember the quick trip to Denver, Colorado, when Dick surprised them by saying he would drive them out. They drove through the night to go to a Star Wars convention that the girls and a cousin were eager to attend. They appreciated their dad doing that for them. Dick and I took a trip to Florida. It was memorable for me, since we celebrated my 60th birthday with significant and special things on that trip. So that is a very quick synopsis of some of the trips we took over the years. Trips always re-emphasized for us God's great handiwork in His creation, and gave us a little reprieve from the routines of a busy home life. They refreshed us and gave us new enthusiasm, for Dick at his workplace and for me at home.

Now moving on to some parenting thoughts. When our children are babies and toddlers, the problems are usually smaller problems. It seems when they mature and grow up, move on to high school, then in college the problems can become bigger. But I feel as children learn to face problems, difficulties, and challenges, their parents also grow and mature in learning how to meet the challenges and dilemmas of being parents. We always hope we are being the best parents possible. In fact, when the kids were teenagers, except for Alicia who was 12 years, I made a short family survey for them to fill out. I wanted to know what areas we needed to improve upon with our parenting responsibilities.

The following were some of the questions I included in my survey . . . Do we as parents spend enough time with you kids? Do we spend enough time with each of you individually? Do we do enough group things as a family? Are we good examples to you? Are we fair? Are we being supportive of each of you? At least they all gave us positive answers, and said we were doing all right in our parenting role. I think it is good for parents to step back and evaluate how things are going with each child.

Dick could see how busy I was each day, and he wanted me to have the kids help more around the house. They had their chores to do, and I would try to get them to help as much as I could, but they were very busy also. They had their homework, spelling bees, science fairs, piano practicing, sports, class trips, school plays, Calvinettes (the church girls' club), and later were in the young people's group at church. We need to recognize that children need a balance of play and work.

Parents do need, however, to have their children pitch in and help. The house we all lived in and enjoyed needed everyone to help with the work and chores. The parent who makes sure their children learn to take on responsibilities is communicating something much different from the parent who lets his son or daughter sit in front of the TV, or play with his smartphone while the mother or father takes on all the work themselves. Children are part of the family and when they help out it does not mean they have to be paid for every little thing. When we grew up on our small farm, we learned to work and to do a job well at a young age. There was always a lot of work to do, and it was important that everyone pitched in and helped. I am afraid things may be changing in some families nowadays; children are not always taught to work and be responsible. When they get older and maybe land a job, they do not give their employer a good day of work . . . they just do not seem to know how to work.

Our girls were able to find summer jobs at a young age which I think was good. The first thing the older two did was sell cards for several years to earn some money. We often would have yard sales, since we were in a good location on a main road; the girls would sell some of their toys and clothing and make a little money. Then the oldest had her first real, regular paying job when she was 11 years old---she delivered a small paper called the Freeway on Mondays after school. They paid her seven cents a copy. She had about 52 customers in our town of New Era which included the businesses where she could leave a bundle of papers. Throughout the years, this job remained in the Walhout family and it was passed on down to all four girls. Other jobs included asparagus and cherry picking, babysitting several days a week, painting the fence for many years at Country Dairy where Dick worked (as well as other jobs there), working at my cousin's tree farm shearing trees, counting trees, and at Christmastime making wreaths. The town gas station hired the two older girls for various jobs there. As they grew older, Alicia worked a summer at McDonalds one year, and many summers were spent working at a grocery store in Hart (11 miles from New Era) for Nichole and Alicia. All these jobs helped them learn how to save money, put in a good day's work, and be responsible. All the girls had enough money saved up to buy their first car (good used ones), and later it went to help pay for a college education. They all also had part time jobs at college and their earnings went towards their college expenses.

Raising a family in a small town meant our kids could walk or ride their bikes to school and to church for various functions. The only drawback was the 30-mile trip to Muskegon when they went to the Christian high school. But we still preferred living in a small town close to both sets of parents, and close to the country. I asked the two youngest to write a paragraph or so on growing up in a small town; I thought it would be interesting to hear it from their perspective. This is what Alicia, the youngest wrote:

> In recollecting about growing up in a small town, rural New Era, I have many fond memories of various functions and activities that have shaped my childhood and who I am. My parents gave my sisters and me a healthy amount of freedom to explore God's creation: like playing by the creek, biking the new rail trail, making pine needle forts from our big white pine tree, and traipsing through the woods behind our house. Because we had parents that liked to give us experiences, they would take us swimming at Lake Michigan, Stony or Silver Lake, snowmobiling through the beautiful Michigan countryside, or morel mushroom hunting at the Walhout farm. We spent lots of time at both sets of grandparents' farms---playing kick the can with cousins or looking for Indian beads, and sometimes biking or walking part of the way there with our dad. I value the foundations of faith I received at New Era Christian School and New Era Christian Reformed Church, and also the sports, plays and musicals, and church youth activities that I was a part of. Even though I had to ride many long hours on my mom's bus when I went off to

high school in Muskegon, I never wished I could live in a bigger city with more attractions or conveniences. I was content with small town life and the family and friends God blessed me with. Now my husband and I enjoy visiting New Era a couple times a year to pass on the value of a special small town to our children. [Alicia, Ryan, and their five children reside in Sioux Falls, South Dakota].

Nichole, the second youngest writes:

I always look back fondly at growing up in the small town of New Era. I had three sisters to play with. There were certain things that all four of us would do together in our house upstairs and sometimes in the family room downstairs. We would set up our Barbie dolls or paper dolls. We had a way we always liked to play, each in our own rooms, but then coming in the hallway to do things together. Our parents would let us keep this mess up for weeks. Especially nice was the sliding pocket door downstairs that could just be pulled closed on the family room. There were tons of games we played. I especially remember playing the card game "Spit" with all four of us. Outside, we liked to play forts in the woods behind our house; we each had our own area to develop. In the fall it was pine needle forts in the side yard. In the winter it was sledding down the neighbor's hill and making snow forts. All of these activities could be played together as sisters, but we often had one or more friends from the town join us as well.

I liked that we could walk or ride our bikes to our small Christian school across town, or catch a ride on the bus if it was cold or rainy when my mom was the bus driver. I liked that we could walk down to the store to buy a special treat, and later the gas station. I liked that we all had friends to play with within bike-riding distance.

 I especially remember summers and the special things we would do, like "Queen for the Day." Each of us girls would take turns being the Queen which meant we would get to pick a special outing to do for the week, maybe have a friend over, sit in the front seat of the car, and choose [and help make] what we wanted for supper one night. I remember lots of our outings were swimming out at Stony Lake. There is so much I could say about growing up in New Era, but my mom is writing the book and not me, so I will conclude by saying that growing up in New Era was special. Both sets of grandparents were within ten minutes of our house, and we spent lots of time on their farms. We looked forward to Christmastime outings to the huge town of Grand Rapids to go to the malls and see the decorations and lights. There were fun activities at school and church, such as the all-church picnics in the summer. My parents made a wonderful home for us, and nurtured us with faith and love, and I am quite sure a lot of patience as well! [Nichole and her husband Nathan, and four year old David live in Ludington, Michigan. They are a little over 30 miles from New Era. It is nice to have them a little closer as they moved from Jenison, which was over an hour's drive away, around Christmastime 2020.]

  In their high school and college years, the girls were involved in activities that took them farther away from home. Alicia went to Dallas, Texas over one spring break with M.O.S.E.S. which is a Christian organization that tries to help those in need. Their week away was spent doing some painting and construction work, and handing out clothing to the poor. Then all the girls went to a youth convention one or two times to places like California, Colorado, Rhode Island, Wisconsin, and Tennessee. Our church would help fund the trips for the young people who attended, and it was an invaluable experience for them. There would be excellent spiritual-emphasis speakers and lots of music the young people would enjoy. Many would come back saying it was a time of growing and maturing in their faith. Kristi participated in START (Summer Training and Reach-out Team) one year. It was a three week mission program in Yucatan, Mexico. They studied the Bible together, completed building projects, and participated in leading church services. They lived right with the villagers, and it was very primitive. It was a great time and a spiritually rewarding experience.

About this time one girl was working, one was off to college, one would be going in the fall, and only Alicia was home finishing up her high school years. You would think I would have been less busy then, but I still watched sports, musicals, and went to the activities Alicia was involved in (and I drove school bus). In this chapter in my life, however, I became very busy as a caregiver---a new job for me (other than taking care of my family members). Once my mom turned 89 years (and before this too) she had problems with dementia. Dad had passed away almost ten years prior, and a niece had been living with Mom from then on, so she did not have to be alone at night. Gradually, it became evident that Mom needed more help, so between hiring a caregiver and my help, we watched over her during the daytime when my niece was at work. In the summer of 1997 things kept getting worse, and it became difficult for me. I would have to run out to Mom's once and often twice a day to care for her (she lived 5 1/2 miles away). My other sisters lived too far away, one in Tennessee and one in California. My siblings said it was time for Mom to go into a nursing home, but I wanted to keep her in her own home as long as possible. I had to do things when caring for her that I never thought I would have to do. My trips out there every day started in April. I had to encourage her to eat, give baths, and change bedding to list a few things. I still did not want to put her in a home; I so hated to do that . . . she was my mom! It got to the point, however, that I was in constant fear of going out to her home and finding her fallen on the floor. So it was time she went into the home, but it still was an awful hard decision for me. The others had said it was up to me when I decided I could not take care of her anymore. When that time came, August 6th, 1997, I had my brother and sister-in-law move her into the home; I just could not do it. I just hated seeing her there in the county home and about cried myself to sleep over it for the first week. I did not like visiting her up there. She was so confused. After a couple of months, I do not even think she realized where she was and what "her home" was anymore. I just felt so sorry for my mom. If the other two sisters had lived closer by, we could have taken turns and maybe kept her in her own home longer. But they did not, and the decision had to be made. Her dementia worsened as the months went on, and it probably did not even matter to her that she was in the Hart home anymore. Why am I including this in my book? We all will likely have to face trials, tribulation, hard decisions, and heartaches at different times in our lives. When difficulties arise it sometimes requires a turn in the road. Your life is not over; it is just taking a turn and you may be heading in a new direction. So it was another different chapter for me---my dad had passed away and my mom was in a home. She was only there less than a year and passed away a month after her 90th birthday.

I called that time in 1997 my traumatic summer with putting mom in the nursing home, and also dealing with an ulcer on my leg. The sore did not want to heal, so there were many trips to Muskegon to see a specialist, and it took numerous weeks to heal. I was limping and in a lot of pain at times and in discomfort. One more difficult thing that summer was sending our second youngest, Nichole, off to college. It was always hard for me when my children started "using their wings and flying from their nest." Me, the "mother bird" missed them a lot, and it was always a hard transition for me. At least she chose Cornerstone University in Grand Rapids (70 miles away), so she could come home often on weekends, which she did.

Maybe by writing about putting Mom in a home and having to make transitions in my life, I can be an encourager to someone going through troubles and problems in their own lives right now. In Ecclesiastes 3:1 we read, "There is a time for everything, and a season for every activity under heaven." Verse 4 says, "A time to weep and a time to laugh, a time to mourn and a time to dance." So all through life we face our ups and downs, happiness and discouragement, days when things are going well, and days when things are not going well. When we entrust our lives completely to God, He gives us strength to face the challenges, the courage to face any affliction, and the wisdom to live a godly life. Even today someone may be hurting, distraught, or have a heart that is breaking. At times like these when in need, we can cry out to Him. We can claim Psalm 121:2, "My help comes from the Lord, the Maker of heaven and earth." When others are down and need encouragement we need to step in and see if we can help. I Thessalonians 5:11 says, "So encourage each other and build each other up." (Living Bible).

This poem I wrote sums up what I have been saying:

Rest On Our Savior's Help and Strength

Sometimes life is so very difficult
    And things just seem to go all wrong . . .
Pain, sorrows, hurts, illnesses come
    And we are not always able to be strong.

The billowing storms come rolling in
    And the sun fails to shine.
The fog completely covers all,
    And there is so much turmoil among mankind.

We try hard to get to the mountain top---
    We work, climb, and do our best.
But then a struggle, a burden tears us down,
    We have no comfort or rest.

We must cope with the struggles . . .
    They are all part of life along our way.
We need to rest on our Savior's help and strength
    To meet the hardships of each day.

We cannot do it on our own

  No matter how very hard we try!
We are only humans, weak and frail
  Badly in need of much help from on high!

We have promises in God's Word
  That He will be beside us and in our heart.
We must turn our problems over to Christ
  And let Him do His essential part.

He promises help, grace, mercy,
  Guidance, strength, protection, and love.
Let's put complete faith and trust in Him
  And turn our turmoil over to Him above.
    (November 6, 2018)

SUGGESTIONS, INDONESIA, HEARTACHES

"Praise be to the God and Father of our Lord Jesus Christ, the Father of compassion and the God of all comfort, who comforts us in all our troubles, so that we can comfort those in any trouble with the comfort we ourselves have received from God" (II Corinthians 1:3-4).

A lady who read my first book, *A Farm Girl's Memories,* said I should write a sequel and include about raising our four daughters. Again, we certainly do not feel we have all the answers as parents, but we learned a lot along the way, and I will include some suggestions. Many of you may be in the teenage stage right now raising your own families. Having teenagers in the home can be a very special time, or it can be a complex and frustrating time, both for the parents and for the children. Some of the things that parents may have to face are arguing, fighting, disagreements, kids being disrespectful, testing of authority, and the constant need of help and advice. But you will get through it, as we did, and that period in our lives when all the kids are living at home is a very special time also. You need to say "no" when it is necessary, and keep burning gas to run them places while they are still under your roof. There may be disagreements between parents and their teenagers over what events they can drive to, when they should come home, dances, what movies to watch, or what functions they should be allowed to attend. Sometimes we would have to say to them, "I know you feel we are wrong here, but we have to do what we feel is right as parents." It is okay to be the unpopular parents and to say no and to stick to your convictions. It can be a hard thing to do though when it would be easier just to give in to their wishes.

We need to reinforce in our teenagers that our hearts, our priorities, and our lives should belong to our faithful Savior, Jesus Christ. That goes along with a sermon I remember when our pastor said if we listen to the wrong kind of music, watch the wrong TV shows and movies, watch the wrong things on the internet, that is what fills our minds and hearts- - - unwholesome and corrupt thoughts. I mentioned previously how important it is to fill our minds and hearts instead with God's Word, good and valuable music, good thoughts and messages from sermons or Christian radio, so that those are the thoughts that are ever in our minds throughout the day. I know for me personally when listening to the words of good Christian songs and hymns, I can feel so uplifted and inspired. There's a song that says, "Heaven came down and glory filled my soul." Maybe that best describes how I often feel when moved by certain songs and how they so touch my heart!

It is vitally important to be spiritually mature and filled with God. If we become empty, Satan will move into the empty house (our hearts), and we do not want that to happen! We need to live each day as unto the Lord seeking to be kind, unselfish, helpful, considerate, trustworthy, pure, contented, and to pray continuously. Pray what it says in Psalm 51:10 and maybe make it your prayer every morning, "Create in me a new, clean heart, O God, filled with clean thoughts and right desires" (Liv. Bible). And in Philippians 4:8 we read, "Finally, brothers, whatever is true, whatever is noble, whatever is right, whatever is pure, whatever is lovely, whatever is admirable---if anything is excellent or praiseworthy---think about such things." How much better the world could be if people put this into practice. Also, remember, "The Lord does not look at the things man looks at. Man looks at the outward appearance, but the Lord looks at the heart" (I Samuel 16:7).

Another thing to impress on our teenagers is "The Lord will work out His plans for their lives" (and ours) as stated in Psalm 138:8 (Liv. Bible). Also, in Psalm 139:16 we read, "You saw me before I was born and scheduled each day of my life before I began to breathe. Every day was recorded in Your Book!" (Liv. Bible). The Old Testament shows over and over how God planned every little detail in the lives of the Israelites. We too should allow Him to plan and control every detail of our lives. He wants to rule over and take care of us in "every little thing." If God thought we were important enough to schedule each day of our lives before we were born, He thinks we are pretty special, and we should make sure our teenagers know that they are special too. Encourage them to put God first in their lives and allow Him to lead them in the plans He has for them. If we follow God's plans it will be so wonderful to be able to say with the Psalmist in chapter 44:18, "Our hearts have not deserted You! We have not left Your path BY A SINGLE STEP" (Liv. Bible). This should be our prayer!

We put a lot of miles on the cars during the girls' teenage years running back and forth for sports, band, choir, plays, and activities with their friends. We chose to send them to the Christian high school 30 miles away and felt we needed to support the kids in as many extra things as we could. Sometimes, they made their best friends when they were involved in a team sport.

One more thing we were firm about is our Sunday worship services. Our church always had services twice on Sundays, and we expected them to attend both services. We just felt it was so important not to let the world seep in on Sundays. Our girls had chances to play on good soccer and basketball teams during the summers, but we had to say "no" to this since it meant missing church. We wanted them to get jobs during their summers that did not involve work on Sundays, which they did.

To me, one of the best sources for raising children is Dr. James Dobson's books. He has written many books on the subject of child-rearing, and they are excellent. You can also get his DVDs on this subject that are so helpful. I have empathy for parents nowadays trying to raise their children in the nurture and admonition of the Lord. The world seems to keep drifting farther and farther from the ways of the Lord with more and greater temptations as the years continue on. So many groups are driven to destroy the family, and schools are not free to teach Christ-centered beliefs and principles. Instead, sexual immorality might be taught at a young age. What can parents and grandparents do to protect our children and teens? Teach them about Christ from little on, keep telling them about the plan of salvation, and pray for them daily. It is a constant battle protecting our children, and we do not want Satan with his temptations to win. We need God's protection and power, along with His *mighty angels* to step in to fight and help protect our children and grandchildren. I wrote a poem back in 1968 that goes along with the temptations young people are facing (I better make it clear first that I never drank):

ONLY A LITTLE

A little act, not so very wrong;
A little word, not so very strong;
    A little temptation, but I gave in;
    After all, it was just a little sin
I thought as I began to drift along.

Come have a drink was the plea,
We'll have some fun . . . wait and see.
    I guess I will, I heard myself say;
    There'll be no harm done anyway
Forgetting that I was hurting me.

On Sunday morn Mom said, come with us;
You need to, honey, please don't fuss.
    Why go to church? I had enough;
    After all, it's just little kids stuff
Said a once tender heart now filled with lust.

Why did I so oft' become mad
And get a kick out of making others sad?
    Could it be that I've turned away?
    Maybe Mom was right the other day.
No . . . it couldn't be . . . I'm not so very bad.

LITTLE ANGELS AND MIGHTY ANGELS

A day later and in a hospital bed;
Again I had followed when the others led.
    We were drunk and had a car,
       Only this time we went much too far.
Oh, why didn't I listen to what my mom said.

The speedometer really shot up in our crate,
And we didn't see the other car till too late.
    It all seemed like such a horrid dream
      When I heard the girl's loud, piercing scream.
Satan sure knows who to choose for bait.

God, as I lay here about to die;
I don't deserve You hearing my cry.
    Five souls forever lost
      Because I failed to count the cost
When the price of "a little" was so very high.

My poem emphasizes what can happen when a person has a little drink, experiments with drugs, looks at a little pornography, swears in order to act cool---and a young person may think it is "just a little sin." But that can lead to someone giving in to more and more until as in the poem, it may be too late---souls forever lost because a person failed to count the cost of what could happen as a result of what they were becoming involved in. It all comes back to what kind of choices you are making. Choices are all so important . . . the first choice, the second one, and then another. They all will lead to something else. You need to think ahead and decide what the choice is going to do to you and how it might affect others. Think . . .would my folks approve of this choice, or would my friends, or my siblings? What about God, would He approve of what I am thinking about doing? The choices young people make will eventually mold them into who they are as individuals. Choices will form their personality and character. Are the choices they are making going to help make their character one of thoughtfulness, kindness, love, sympathy, cheerfulness OR will their character be made up of anger, bitterness, selfishness, harshness, and impatience?

What better way for a teenager to learn to make their best choices than from the examples of their parents, extended family, grandparents, Christian schools, involvement with a good Bible believing church, and going to Christian colleges. The majority of children acquire the characteristics and habits of their parents. Isn't it surprising when you hear your little toddlers saying some of the words and expressions you use, or mimicking some of your habits? So you have to make sure you are being a good role model to them and that you are a good example all the time. You cannot tell them one thing and then live a different way. They may be following your footsteps some day; make sure they are worthy footsteps to follow.

There are many who have helped us grow spiritually along life's way. If you think back, you realize how deeply people have affected you as you were growing up. I cannot emphasize enough how important it is to teach your children over and over about Christ and the way to salvation---from toddlers on up. That is our main goal in life---that our children become followers of Christ. I John 5:21 from the Living New Testament translation says, "Dear children, keep away from anything that might take God's place in your hearts." That means God must be foremost in our hearts, in our children's and grandchildren's hearts, and the hearts of others. You only have them living with you under the same roof for so long, and then they will be out on their own. That time will go faster than you think! I wrote this down once about time passing so quickly and will share it:

> I did a very difficult thing this past Monday . . . left the baby of the family, Alicia, 14 hours away at Dordt College in Iowa. Well, really two difficult things---a daughter was married the day before we had to leave for Iowa (the first of our daughters to marry). She is living only 30 minutes away so that will be okay. Again, as with the previous three daughters, it is always difficult for me to send my daughters off to college. It has been a struggle for me all this week leaving Alicia so far away, like losing a best friend. Thankfully, my daughter is happy at college and is adjusting easily. That makes me feel somewhat better and knowing that she is not homesick makes me glad, but I still feel saddened over my youngest daughter leaving home and being so far away. I know my college daughter has been seeking God's leading in her life, so I have peace in her decision, and she has my blessing, but it still is hard on me! But then I think . . . when the mother robin loses all her babies from her nest, does she go on singing and praising Him from sunrise to sunset? I believe the answer is probably yes! I know we should not dwell on our difficulties. There are others with really huge problems and struggles. We have so much to be thankful for! We need to be like the mother robin and keep praising Him! Our God is an awesome God! I am reminded that if we can be happy and content with the little things of life, we can be happy indeed.

Our priority is our children's faith, but we also must be a witness to others. Sometimes we tend to think it is too great of a responsibility . . . how is it even possible? I will quote from the devotional book I wrote:

> The whole responsibility is not on us totally, nor is the final outcome up to us. We just need to get busy and plant the seeds---perhaps by being a good listener, encouraging someone when they are feeling down and sharing about the hope we can have in Christ, or by passing on a favorite Bible verse. It may even be something like walking away from gossip or dirty jokes, or making a comment like "I do not like you swearing, and you are taking the Lord's name in vain." We can stand up for what we believe by just a word or a couple sentences, or just by our example. The way we conduct ourselves by being truthful, responsible, having high morals, and portraying Christ's love may all be seeds planted. And then after we plant, pray! A speaker on the radio told of all the people he regularly prays for . . . unsaved neighbors, unsaved friends, unsaved relatives, the grocery clerk, the postmaster . . . there are so many we should be praying for! So two very important things anyone can do---plant seeds and pray, and God will do His part to bring the lost sheep into the fold. Sometimes serving God means doing hundreds of "little things" day by day. By being faithful in the little things, we can be used by God. We will have the opportunities if we are willing to do our part. God can make everything fall into place, and the result will be a harvest of souls for Him. Our job may only be planting the seeds, someone else may water and provide nourishment, God will add the rain and the sunshine, and another may bring the

harvest in. Our part is to keep sowing seeds, keep our priorities straight, and keep trying to make a difference in our lives and in the lives of others. God gives His love to us freely; we in turn need to reflect this love and be sensitive to others' needs, trials, burdens, and difficulties. It is easy to get discouraged at the way things are progressing in the world . . .pornography, sexual sins, same-sex marriage, a Christian judge thrown out of office because of his stand for the Ten Commandments, abortions, killings, marital unfaithfulness---to name a few. The only way it will ever change is for people to come to know God.

As we face each new day, remember that "Every day is a gift." We need to try and be purposeful as we face the new day and use opportunities to serve God. Maybe we can perform a small act of kindness to a lonely neighbor, bring a meal to a shut-in, make a phone call of encouragement, write a get well card, drive a person who is not able to drive, speak kind words to someone, or let others know you care about them. You may think that it is such a little thing, but God can use it and bless it. Colossians 3:12 states, "Therefore, as God's chosen people, holy and dearly loved, clothe yourselves with compassion, kindness, humility, gentleness and patience." And in verse 14, "Over all these virtues put on love, which binds them all together in perfect unity." So we need to watch for opportunities and not let them slip through our fingers or pass us by. We are presented with countless opportunities to serve God day by day.

I was so thankful that I could be a "stay at home" mother; it was important to us when raising our girls. Foremost, I wanted to be with my girls all I could. It was difficult realizing how quickly the children were growing and how they soon would be leaving our home. I mentioned when our oldest went off to college 14 hours away, it was a traumatic time for me, but she made the transition easier than I did. She really liked going to college! But for me, it was difficult to see them go off to college; I liked having my whole family's feet under my kitchen table for meals - - - for us to be together! Another thing we thought was important, if possible, was to have our children attend Christian colleges: to be taught from a Christian perspective, have good people mentoring them, and make other good Christian friends. Being at Christ-based colleges might help them avoid becoming mixed up with the wrong friends or being exposed to unbiblical teachings in liberal colleges.

Then came the chapter in my life of the girls getting married . . . again, it was difficult for me as a couple of them settled so far away. Then the grandchildren came along, and it was hard with 10 of our 11 grandchildren so far away, in South Dakota and Texas. We love spending time with children and grandchildren, but it is harder to do this when it is a 14-hour drive and a 22-hour drive away (including stops). Families who have your immediate family close by, be ever thankful for this! I know we have to accept that each child needs to settle where their husband finds work, but it does not make it any easier. Our daughters are very good at trying to keep us current with the grandchildren's activities. We talk on the phone often, email and use Skype, but we still feel we miss out on a lot being so far away!

A nice thing we did several times over a spring break was have the whole family come from all different directions and meet up for an extended weekend. Those were just the best times of fun, fellowship, and renewing times with grandchildren and the rest of the family. We stayed in Davenport, Iowa for the first meeting place. One time we met in Milwaukee and went on the downtown riverwalk, to a museum, zoo, bowling, and out to eat. Another time the location was Chicago, and we saw lots of things in that big city. Those times were so priceless, making special memories with the family. I encourage those of you with young children still at home to take time to do things together. Watch out . . . that time while the whole family is together will speed by so very quickly and the next thing you know, some will be off to college or getting married!

 I mentioned the Texas family. We maybe did not fully realize how good we had it when they lived in North Muskegon, only 20 minutes from us. We frequently enjoyed dropping in there for a visit, and they would often come our way for Sunday dinners. Those were wonderful days when we could spend a lot of time with them! We were privileged to experience the joy of three children born to them while they lived in our area. We enjoyed having the grandchildren stay overnight at our house many times. We would pick them up and take them to playgrounds which they always liked to do and did many other fun things with them. Grandchildren were another new chapter in our lives, and we totally loved it! Maybe getting old is not so nice, but when you can have grandchildren, it helps make being old feel more worthwhile.

 As parents, we tried to encourage our children to be mission-minded. When our Texas daughter, Kristi, first started a friendship with Jeff, he was involved in missions---in Africa. In fact, she even made a trip with Jeff's folks to visit him while he was still in Togo, Africa. Jeff has a degree in computers and after they were married, he took an IT job in Muskegon. It was during this time that we were able to spend a lot of time with them. However, that was about to change. Jeff and Kristi were always interested in missions with the possibility of serving in that way together. We were sad to hear (sometime in 2009) that if they could raise the needed missionary support, they were going to Indonesia where there was a need for a network administrator. But we were proud of them too, that they were willing to answer God's call. That is what we always taught and influenced our children to do, but did they have to go so far away and take our three precious little grandchildren with them? And for such a long time?

We had to say good-bye to Jeff and Kristi and the kids the afternoon of July 27th, 2010 for three long years---one of the hardest days of our married lives! To watch them go through security, turn around and wave good-bye one last time before boarding the plane was terribly difficult! I get teary-eyed just thinking about it again. And I can imagine how hard it was for them leaving everyone and everything behind! Three years is way too long for family to be absent from one another---three years gone forever from one another's lives. Time with family and loved ones become so precious as we keep getting older. May God allow us many wonderful years yet with a good quality of life so we can enjoy one another and our wonderful family.

They boarded the plane for the arduous journey of about 48 hours of flying and waiting around in airports. The kids did well traveling all that time, except poor five-year-old Daniel had motion sickness half of the time when they were in planes for almost 24 hours! How tiring the 13 1/2 hour flight was for them from Los Angeles to Taiwan!

After finally arriving in Indonesia, it was a busy time for Jeff and Kristi. They needed to find a house, the necessary household items to set up a home, and bikes for transportation around town. They were also preparing for the children to attend a new school while they began language school. Then August 16 was another terribly difficult day of our lives, even more so for Jeff and Kristi and the kids! Jeff called Dick in the morning and notified us that Kristi had a miscarriage at 18 weeks along. What a sad thing in a strange country with them not yet knowing the language or who to call for help in the middle of the night when she started to miscarry. After losing the baby, Jeff and Kristi closed the door, sat, and grieved while holding their little boy. The kids, ages 7, 5, and 3, were also very sad to learn of the loss of their brother. Anna drew a picture of the little baby and wrote, "He was going to be so cute but now he's gone. We will miss him." Someone must have gotten the kids off to school the next day, and someone must have taken them to the hospital to translate as Kristi had to have a D & C. Here they had only been there two and a half weeks and to have all this happen! They named the little boy Micah Abram. It was so hard having them so far away and feeling there was nothing we could do to help. I truly believe sometimes a mother can feel a strong tie or bond with their daughter. It was something . . . all Sunday I felt down, tired, and depressed and did not know why. I usually feel pretty happy and content. Even late afternoon and later in the evening I just felt like having a good, hard cry but could not put my finger on why! Then we got the call early the next morning informing us of the miscarriage. Perhaps that is why I was feeling so sad on Sunday, and especially later in the afternoon and evening when I felt so down. Maybe I was experiencing Jeff and Kristi's grief of what they were going through. . .the mother and daughter's close relationship (time difference there of 13 hours ahead). I just felt so bad for Jeff and Kristi, especially as a mother---the way it hurt me, I could not imagine how much they were hurting. We felt at such a loss as to what to do. Dick wrote the following in an email, "How do you respond after a day like today. I guess it points out to me more than ever how we are not the ones in control. But we know the One who is! And He is strong and powerful and kind and gentle and loving---and in control today and forever. We place this little one into His strong arms for care and protection that we cannot give him now. We also know what the future holds and look forward to meeting one who has had the privilege of being held in the strong arms of the Savior who is kind and gentle and loving. I pray that He will demonstrate His healing power to you, Jeff and Kristi and kids, in the days ahead and make clear to all of us, His kindness, gentleness and love. Love you, Dad."

Why do I include such a sad story in a book? Maybe it can be a help to someone else who maybe now is going through a difficult trial, heartache, grief, sorrow, pain, or sadness. No matter what happens in life, what happens tomorrow, or the next day, or the next week, or the next month . . . we rest in God's love, care, protection, and in His hands.

Jeff and Kristi became busy with language study in Indonesia and settling into a home. Then around their first Christmas there, Kristi had another miscarriage. As the months continued on, they thought all was going well when she became pregnant again, and they were so relieved to pass the 18 weeks of Micah Abram's passing. But another tragedy for them, and they lost another little boy at 23 weeks. He was named Isaac Mark and had appeared to be a healthy little baby; but the doctor thought that with the baby's activity the cord had become too twisted, cutting off the oxygen and nutrients. It again was a very, very painful time for all of us! It was helpful that Dick and our oldest daughter were able to be there for a visit two weeks after this happened, with tickets they had bought months ahead. I did not dare go as I would not be able to stand such long flights---one of them 15 and a half hours! I also was afraid the flying might trigger some dizzy spells again for me that had finally quit occurring. Even my husband said after three hours on that long flight, he wanted to parachute out of the plane! He said he hated the brutal and exhausting experience of the long flights. At least it was nice for Jeff and Kristi's family to have some company during those three years of being in Indonesia. Another daughter and husband made the trip in February, then Dick and daughter as mentioned in September, and Jeff's folks visited them when they moved to Papua, Indonesia.

Jeff and Kristi had to face many challenges while serving the Lord in Indonesia. Daniel came down with a very serious case of malaria, and Jeff became seriously ill with dengue-fever. James had a bout with malaria and one time hit his head hard when he fell off a neighbor's trampoline onto cement! Little Rachel, during their second term (will tell more about her later), had some frightening asthma attacks as a baby. There were so many real concerns, and we were worrying and praying here at home when they were going through all those troubled waters. We were so elated and happy when their three-year term was up, they came back to the United States, and we could see them again---with their three children all of a sudden three years older!

The highlight then of 2013 was when they came home on furlough. They had to put up with the long trip again---46 hours of either being in planes or waiting around in airports, the longest flight was 14 and a half hours! We were so jubilant to see them again and to have them close by and away from all those tropical diseases for a while. And the good news, Kristi was pregnant again and was able to give birth while they were in the U.S. Little Rachel Abigail was born on August 27th, two years from the very day they had lost Isaac Mark. What a miraculous way that God was providing healing for Jeff and Kristi, and they called Rachel "God's precious gift!" Rachel was and still is such a blessing! During furlough they could stay with Jeff's folks in Spring Lake, since they have extra living quarters for guests in the lower level of their home. This was 40 miles from us, and we took advantage of seeing Jeff and Kristi and our four grandchildren as much as we possibly could while they were in Michigan. It was so nice having them around while they were on their furlough!

Furlough came to an end much too quickly and it was another very difficult day of once again saying our good-byes, watching them go through security, and waving those last good-byes. Their second term was shorter, though, since Rachel struggled with asthma due to the smoke pollution in Sentani and the open-air homes. Therefore, they made the hard decision of leaving Papua, Indonesia and filling a different need at the International Linguistic Center in Dallas, Texas.

It was so good to have them near us again for a while in Michigan. They had preparations to make and housing to find in Texas before moving there. We had a bittersweet Christmas in 2016. Sweet since the whole family (19 of us) would be together once again for Christmas! It was rather bitter and sad over the holidays, since Jeff and Kristi and children would be moving to Dallas, Texas on December 29 to start work there. I traveled down with them and stayed a few days to help them clean and settle in, and returned by Amtrak. So changes again for their family, but we were very thankful they were in the United States and that we could see them occasionally throughout the year.

    I reflect on that time in their lives, and it reminds me how we all are traveling on this journey of life. It is so amazing to me how God has put EACH and every one of us here on earth at this particular time in history to fulfill the very purpose and plan He has for each one of us---and He knows each of us by name! No one else can fulfill this plan He has for ME. While we are navigating down His path there will be ups and downs, happiness and heartaches, joys and sorrows, easy times and troubling times, laughter and tears, times of death, and times to be born. But through it all . . . He is right there walking beside us! The song "God Will Take Care of You" comes to mind---because through every day and over all the way on our journey on this earth, He promises He will take care of us! And I know during those painful and difficult experiences for Jeff and Kristi and kids in Indonesia, they would say they were so thankful they could lean on the Lord for comfort, love, strength, and peace to get through it all. Jeff and Kristi also say they are grateful for the friendships and relationships they were able to develop while there. They enjoyed getting to know the culture and the people, and they felt blessed to have helped play a part in bringing God's word to the Bibleless people groups of Indonesia.

We all at some time in our life on this earth will experience sadness, pain, illness, heartaches, and trials. We do not always understand why and sometimes the burdens seem too great to bear. We can be assured, however, of God's wonderful promises in His Holy Word . . . He will be with us and see us through! We read of these promises in the following two verses, "The Lord is close to the brokenhearted and saves those who are crushed in spirit. A righteous man may have many troubles, but the Lord delivers him from them all" (Psalm 34:18 -19). Also, very comforting verses in II Corinthians 4:17-18 where we read, "These troubles and sufferings of ours are, after all, quite small and won't last very long. Yet this short time of distress will result in God's richest blessing upon us forever and ever! So we do not look at what we can see right now, the troubles all around us, but we look forward to the joys in Heaven which we have not yet seen. The troubles will soon be over, but the joys to come will last forever" (Living N.T.). What a marvelous and glorious promise in that last short sentence! May it be a comfort to someone this very day!

BLESSINGS, GRANDCHILDREN, DAVID

"Every good and perfect gift is from above, coming down from the Father of the heavenly lights, who does not change like shifting shadows" (James 1:17).

The Lord promises to be with us through our heartaches and to walk alongside us each step of the way. God also gives us wonderful blessings over and over, day by day. Are we thankful for them each day? Sometimes we need to just take time to stop and think of all the beautiful things, the blessings that God puts in the world for us to enjoy. Look around you . . . stars shining forth in the darkest night, beautiful sunsets in the evening hour, a rainbow in the sky, springtime with budding leaves and flowers, the ocean's blue-green churning waves, cows grazing on grassy hills, even the powerful storms, the hummingbirds flying from flower to flower, butterflies with their delicate wings, a creek winding along with babbling sounds, squirrels scampering around tree trunks, and the birds that sing, to name a few.

Our foremost and greatest blessing, however, is to have salvation full and free and to go to Heaven when we die. John 3:36 clearly states, "Whoever believes in the Son has eternal life, but whoever rejects the Son will not see life, for God's wrath remains on him." So it is indeed a blessing for those who accept Christ, but not for those who do not. When our life on this earth is over we either go to Heaven or to Hell. Those are the only two possibilities. We will not remain buried in a grave beside a tombstone. We cannot enter Heaven simply because we are a good person. Romans 3:12 says, "There is no one who does good, not even one." Or in Ecclesiastes 7:20 we read, "There is not a righteous man on earth who does what is right and never sins." Read the Bible, and you will find references where Hell is a terrible place of suffering forever and ever, darkness; it is so horrible that you do not want to spend an eternity there! That would be so unbearable and dreadful! Are you absolutely certain where you will be going? You can be, if you accept the Lord Jesus as your Savior, ask for forgiveness of your sins, and then live to walk in His ways and serve Him.

We all have many possessions, and some things we treasure such as sports, hobbies, nice homes, expensive cars, recreational toys, vacations, and you can add to this list. But none of these have any real and lasting value! Luke 12:34 says, "Wherever your treasure is, there your heart and thoughts will also be" (Liv. New Testament). It is our very souls that are priceless! They are God's treasure, and the only thing we can take from earth to Heaven. As the verse says, if the wrong treasures become first in our lives, then that is where our heart is and that is wrong. In this world there are really only two groups---the saved group or the unsaved group. Which of the two groups do you belong to?

A few years ago we were on a trip when we received word at different times that three people in our church were diagnosed suddenly with different types of serious cancer. Thankfully, they all were treated and are doing well today. We are often reminded how short life can be when a sudden death happens due to an illness or an accident. Just this last week we had a terrible tragedy in our community, a half of a mile from us. A little five-year-old girl died in a choking accident, a heartbreaking incident. For all of us, time is slipping away. Job 8:9 says, "Our days on earth are but a shadow." Another version of the Bible says, "Our days here on earth are as fleeting [transient] as shadows." It is an interesting and significant way of putting it, but a bit scary too! Life is fleeting---lasting only for a short time! Even at the age I am now, I look back and think, "Where has the time gone?" The days and the weeks continue to fly by so swiftly! Thus, it is important not to delay this very day and make sure you have the right treasures and that your heart is right with God! We look around at the bustling world. Do other people know what the real treasure is? We should not be so concerned with material belongings and other time-consuming possessions, but be concerned instead about winning souls before it is too late. Matthew 6:19-20 instructs, "Do not store up for yourselves treasure on earth, where moth and rust destroy, and where thieves break in and steal. But store up for yourselves treasures in Heaven, where moth and rust do not destroy." I wrote in my devotional booklet, "Let us pray diligently and fervently this week that we make the most of every opportunity to witness for Christ and to bear good fruit. Let us get busy for Him in our actions, in our thoughts, and in our prayers. Allow our Father to show us the work He wants us to do and then let us produce fruit for Him! This is our prayer, Lord, for today . . . to do some good, serve, say something helpful, do a kind deed, help someone, and sow fruitful seed, but we need You to show us how and then give us guidance and strength."

Yes, we have times of suffering on this earth, but many of us also have luxuries and live well. It is important to be grateful to God for these gifts! We also need to watch when we are enjoying these blessings so that we do not become complacent and give God a second or third place love. Is God totally first? God has to be our all in all; we cannot be lukewarm Christians. To help keep our priorities straight, I think of the song, "Lead Me, Guide Me." This is one of my favorite songs. If we allow God to lead us along life's way, we cannot stray from walking with Him. We, as believers, need to walk each day with Him . . . to have Him guide us each and every day, allowing Him to lead us each step and each moment. We also need to read the Bible, maybe attend a Bible Study, attend an evangelical church each Sunday, have good Christian friends, pray diligently, and serve Him by sowing seeds and witnessing when we have the opportunities. Then we should grow and mature in Christ and avoid becoming lukewarm Christians.

I mentioned earlier how important it is to try and make sure your loved ones know the way to salvation. We are so thankful that our daughters and sons-in-law have made that important decision, as well as some of our grandchildren already at young ages. Something we can do as grandparents when we are around our grandchildren is to be good examples and try to reinforce what their parents, Christian schools, and churches are teaching them. I stated before that parents nowadays need all the help they can get when raising their families. Parenting is so challenging today with so many things trying to affect or control children, possibly leading them astray. There may be bad influences at school, friends tempting them in the wrong direction, much coming from the world and the media encouraging wrong actions or thoughts, and ungodly content and temptations on their cell phones that may corrupt their young minds and deceive them.

Again, from the devotional booklet I wrote:

> Satan is always tempting people with worldly pleasures, tempting with his vices and evil doings and many give in to him. When tempted over and over, it is hard for people to be emphatic enough to turn from Satan and instead see what Christ has to offer---sins forgiven and a home in Heaven. The world has nothing that can even begin to compare with a promise like that! People may try to come up with something like a brand new $400,000 home, a fantastic fulfilling job with great wages, prestige and fame, frequent weekend trips and vacations, or popularity and being socially in with the important people of the world. Could these be the pleasures Satan is offering us? They are nothing but "dust," and count for "nothing" when you look at what Christ offers---the forgiveness of sins and to live with Him eternally. Perhaps you are at a crossroad in your life right now. The fact is we will all face the crossroads in life, and we need to make important decisions. When we stand at the crossroad, say "no" to Satan, and try to figure out the way God would want us to take and walk by grace in it.

We have four grandchildren who are already teenagers and have thankfully made good choices so far. It is my hope when all of our grandchildren read this book, as well as other young people, they will think about the preceding chapters. I mentioned this earlier and I am very convinced of its importance. What are young people filling their minds with? Instead of filling their minds with TV and movie garbage, cell phone temptations, unwholesome music, and unacceptable content on the internet, they need to be filled with God's Word, the love of Christ, and delight in worshiping God. Their minds need to be so filled with good thoughts and wholesome content that there will be no room left for bad ideas and bad thoughts to sneak in. They need to be so enthused over their relationship with Christ that they will readily attend church and bring their unchurched friends. To reach this failing and wicked world, it needs to start with our young children. They need to be so filled and bubbling over with Christ that they will be equipped to stand against the wiles of the devil and will desire to pass their faith on. Those of you with young children, remember what a tremendous calling God has given you! I hope some of these things that I have pointed out will be helpful. Ten years down the line I hope and pray our churches will be filled with young families and not so many empty pews!

    I introduced you to Jeff and Kristi's family in the last chapter . . . they have five children who are currently 1, 8, 15, 17, and 19 years old. While they were in Indonesia, they contracted some very serious tropical diseases, and sometimes had to travel on a small motorbike in heavy traffic with children while carrying bags of groceries, among other concerning things. Yet there can be worries when raising children in the United States also. Rachel came down with COVID in Texas when she was seven years old. We all were so concerned for her since she did not want to eat or drink, and was very lethargic. Kristi planned to take her to the hospital the following day if she was not any better. Thankfully, on the next day she started improving, another case of God's protection helping little Rachel through that difficult time!

LITTLE ANGELS AND MIGHTY ANGELS

Mentioning COVID, we were in Texas visiting Jeff, Kristi, and the children March 8 through 13 of 2020. We enjoyed our time there and the coronavirus was just surfacing in the United States. As we drove across the states to the Smoky Mountains, we started to experience what it was like living in the world with the virus. We had bagged breakfasts handed to us at motels, and we were unable to eat in restaurants or use their restrooms. Now, here it is over two and a half years later, and we are still dealing with it. No one would have ever dreamed it would last so long! During the summer of 2020, with more staying home with COVID-19, we took many car rides for something to do. We drove out to Lake Michigan more that summer and fall than any other year in our married life. Two bad memories surface when I think of 2020 . . . the coronavirus, and that whole year I was dealing with so much sciatic pain which had started already in October of 2019. However, good memories overcame the bad memories since that was the year my first book was published (June of 2020) which was so exciting, satisfying, and fulfilling. I give God the praise and glory for that accomplishment!

Now I have some stories about our South Dakota family (Van Der Bills) who have five young children, ages 7, 9, 10, 12, and 13 years old. Maybe their *guardian angels* have to be especially vigilant with these active children when four are boys! One very scary time for the parents, and later when we as grandparents heard about it, was best described in an email from Alicia:

> I am over my shaky feelings and seeing that car hit us every time I shut my eyes. We were hit by a small SUV while on a walk Tuesday night. Ryan was pushing Randy and Rusty in the stroller and the other

two were walking. The car hit the stroller and Adelyn and amazingly, besides a few minor bruises, we are all okay! We were in the right, crossing the crosswalk, and this lady in the SUV turned left and said she did not see us. Once we all calmed down, the woman, who was very emotional, said she had just lost her husband a month ago and has six grandkids. We prayed together, and she went on her way; I hope she is emotionally okay. The kids bounced back very quickly. It took me a little longer to not see it in my mind over and over. We are just so thankful that she stopped when she did, that she was not going too fast, that the stroller did not tip, and all sorts of other things.

It was a very scary thing when Alicia called us and told us about it. We were so very thankful everyone was okay! I think their *mighty angels* were watching over them all on that day!

There was also the time the Van Der Bills were playing in the backyard with extended family. All of a sudden, Randy, who was six at the time, fell off his swing and was bleeding on the top of his head. One look by the parents, and they could see it would be necessary to make a trip to the emergency room at the hospital. Falling out of a swing is one thing, but somehow Randy rolled forward as he fell and hit his head on the deck piling. His dad brought him into the emergency room, and he had to have 12 stitches. Randy was very brave through it all - - - a real trooper! So yes, accidents can happen at home when you least expect it.

Another time the boys were being boys . . . spitting nails out of their mouths as missiles from jets. What shock and alarm had to go through their mom's mind when Randy came out of his bedroom and told her he had swallowed a nail! Again, a trip to the hospital where he had to have several x-rays and a CAT scan. The doctor could see where the nail was and said the best thing to do was wait and see if it would pass on its own since his stomach was not punctured. They sent him home and told him to be more calm and not so rambunctious for a few days. Sure enough, after six days and on Thanksgiving Day, things were successful and Randy did not have to go around anymore with a TWO INCH nail inside of him. That seemed pretty miraculous to us "that it all came out okay," and on Thanksgiving Day!

    I have one more grandson to mention. This is little David who only lives 30 miles away, and we can see him much more often. Of the eleven grandchildren, we have seven grandsons and four granddaughters. And the newest, fourth granddaughter is special because she has recently joined the family through adoption. The Texas family had been hoping to adopt, and little Marielle came to them in a unique way. She had been staying in a foster home since birth, and that family became ill with COVID. Jeff and Kristi were asked to take care of Marielle to protect her while the foster family recovered. They took care of her then, have had her ever since, and the whole family has fallen in love with her. Their court date was in May of 2022 when she became their daughter legally. What a miraculous way God works things out!

    But I had started telling about David, and he has a special story that goes along with his birth. It started in February of 2018 when Nathan and Nichole, the parents, stopped by from a trip up north. They had very exciting news to share---they were expecting after hoping to start a family for almost ten years!

    I remember distinctly when things began to happen since our whole family was together in a restaurant the night before. They were all with us celebrating our 43rd wedding anniversary early, since the Texas and South Dakota families were in Michigan visiting at the time. That night, Nichole's water unexpectedly broke, and the next day (May 8), she was admitted to a hospital in Grand Rapids. They were living in Jenison then and quite close to the major hospitals. The intent was to keep her calm and comfortable in the hospital and give the baby time to grow, since she was only 28 weeks along. Nichole was given steroid shots to help with the baby's lung development, and magnesium to help with brain development. Around 9:45 a.m. on May 12, a nurse happened to be in the room routinely monitoring the baby's vitals when all of a sudden the heart beat dropped. Nichole's doctor and her team just happened to be right outside the door, heard what was happening, and the decision was quickly made to have an emergency c-section. Not 15 minutes later, at 10:22 a.m., Nathan and Nichole were the proud parents of a little baby boy who made his entrance into this world at 28 weeks and 5 days. He weighed in at two pounds and eleven and a half ounces. Some of us were able to see him later that day. You cannot imagine what a tiny little guy he was! A lot of prayers were made on behalf of little David. Many were very concerned about him, but David seemed to progress normally one step at a time. We were not at all familiar with premature births, and since he was so very early, we worried that so much could go wrong. They certainly are equipped at the Helen DeVos Children's Hospital and have incredible nurses and doctors on their staff to care for these tiny babies. Later, when the pathology report came back it showed Nichole's water broke early due to many infections; there were infections in the placenta and umbilical cord, but praise God again, David did not contract any of them! The infections caused some of the blood vessels to be restricted and others to change, which likely would have resulted in David not being able to get any nourishment through the cord if the pregnancy had continued. All were miracles that he came through! We have a lively, healthy, and interesting little four year old!

That summer he was born changed things drastically for Nathan and Nichole. Nichole drove 25 minutes every day to be with David. He spent the next 72 days in the Neonatal Intensive Care Unit at the Helen DeVos Children's Hospital in Grand Rapids. There preemies receive around the clock care from a team of experts. It was nice they were close and David could be at that hospital which is one of the best children's hospitals in the nation! Nathan had to return to work during the day, but he would join Nichole and David evenings. They were taught how to care and handle such a tiny infant. David was finally able to go home on July 22 with a monitor that he wore for the next two months. He weighed six pounds and six ounces when he went home. Then at six months old, he weighed over 15 pounds. What a miracle and yes, I believe God sent His *guardian angels* to watch over David and his parents through it all. I can see God's help in many ways---that the nurse was in the room taking David's vitals at the precise time when his heart rate dropped, that Nichole's doctor and team were there at that very minute outside the door to expedite the emergency c-section so quickly which was so very important, that they could be at one of the best children's hospitals in the nation . . . but did all these things just happen? No, it was all in God's plan that David could be born healthy, that he made it through those 72 days step by step, that he progressed well, and that he thrived when he went home.

What a special story about how God and His *angels* work in our lives on this earth. David is a normal little four year old who is very inquisitive and likes to see how things work. He likes to push buttons, turn on light switches and fans, watch how things work (like Grandpa's coffee maker), and the most amazing thing, name musical selections. Nichole can play the recorded songs on their piano and David can name the songs after just a couple of the notes are played, and he can name many of the composers also. They are not easy songs either, like "Fur Elise" by Beethoven, "Perpetuum Mobile" by Weber, and "Clair de Lune" by Debussy. He can say all the big words correctly and is very advanced in his speech and vocabulary for a four-year-old. David is an eager learner and knows his shapes, letters, numbers, and most of the states since he loves maps. What a joy David is to his parents and to us too, as grandparents; ALL our grandchildren are such a great joy to us! One grandchild out of eleven that we can see almost every week since his family lives close to us.

To grandparents, grandchildren are very special, and all our grandchildren are very special to us! Sometimes we may have a tendency to brag a bit about them, but that is another role of grandparents. Right? Our oldest beautiful and sweet granddaughter is a very good writer already at 19 years and has written some very excellent and meaningful poems. Our eldest grandson is very interested in aviation and in becoming an airline pilot. Another is called our inventor who is very creative and constantly thinking about inventing and making new things. He also enjoys gardening and nature. One loves raptors and knows a lot about them. She also is getting into growing succulent plants and likes watching their progress. Three are so interested in jets, have memorized a great amount of information about them, and like to make models of jets in Dad's workshop and are very good at it! A seven-year-old-grandson is also learning to make items in Daddy's workshop, and is interested in making electrical things. The little eight-year-old granddaughter likes swinging, scooters, her dolls, lots of stuffed animals, and having tea parties. Our newest adopted granddaughter is beautiful, happy, and such a good little baby dearly loved by all! That is a very short synopsis, but I just needed to mention a little about our grandchildren. It is so interesting to watch them grow and mature and see how their interests develop and how their young minds pursue various hobbies and activities. We try our best to keep up with them though they live a great distance away, and we are thankful they come to Michigan to visit when they can. We make the trip to see them too each year. This chapter in our lives as grandparents is very interesting and special indeed!

ANGELS, PROTECTION, RETIREMENT

"Bless the Lord, you *mighty angels* of His who carry out His orders, listening for each of His commands. Yes, bless the Lord, you armies of His *angels* who serve Him constantly. Let everything everywhere bless the Lord. And how I bless Him too!" (Psalm 103:20-22 Liv. Bible).

I think Psalm 91:11-12 is such an exceptional and wonderful passage. I mentioned it earlier since it is very special to me, and I wish to quote it again. We read in the Living Bible, "For He orders His *angels* to protect you wherever you go. They will steady you with their hands to keep you from stumbling against the rocks on the trail." Or I like how it reads in the King James version of the Bible, "They [the *angels*] shall bear you up in their hands, lest you dash your foot against a stone." It is a real comforting promise to me . . . that the *angels* will bear me up in their hands so that I will not even DASH MY FOOT AGAINST A STONE! I think of that verse sometimes when I am walking along on an uneven path, that an *angel* may be right alongside me keeping me from stubbing a toe or tripping. It is so exciting and wonderful to know *angels* are beside us protecting us! We do not always sense the presence of angels in our day to day lives, but God promises it is so for Christians. You can read for yourself about the many happenings and stories about *angels* protecting, caring, and serving God's people in the Bible. Another wonderful promise for Christians is in Hebrews 1:14, "Are not all *angels* ministering spirits sent to serve those who will inherit salvation?" This means the *angels* comply with God's commands on our behalf and provide duties and services for us if we are Christians.

Angels help guide us, guard and protect us, but they cannot lead us to Christ. However, they are exceedingly happy when a person accepts Christ! Jesus says in Luke 15:10, "There is rejoicing in the presence of the *angels* of God over one sinner who repents." Another important job of the *angels* is in Matthew 24:31, "And He will send His *angels* with a loud trumpet call, and they will gather His elect from the four winds, from one end of the heavens to the other." This means when Christ sounds the trumpet or gives the signal, the *angels* will then gather the true believers (God's people) from everywhere on earth (the four winds meaning the four corners of the earth - - - north, south, east, and west). This will be the second coming of Christ. I have pointed out some of the important duties, work, and assignments of the *mighty angels* of God. Their commitment, tasks, and charges are so important---important enough that angels are listed at least 273 times in the Bible. Although they are highly valued and have very important purposes and commissions, they are still under God's commands and orders. We also have a task concerning the *angels* and read, "Do not forget to entertain strangers, for by so doing some people have entertained *angels* without knowing it." (Hebrews 13:2).

What better way to prove the great assignments of the angels than real-life stories. I have listed many that have happened in our lives and in the lives of others in previous chapters. They have all been significant stories and examples of God using His *mighty angels* for protection. I cannot say one story is more relevant than another, but these last two stories are foremost in the minds of my husband and me. Dick's happened in the winter, February of 2001. For many years while Dick worked for Country Dairy, one of his jobs was driving the tank truck. They used that truck to transport the milk from their outlying farms to the milk processing plant on the home farm. Also, once or twice a week they had to run a load of Country Dairy's extra cream up to House of Flavors in Ludington (30 miles away), since House of Flavors bought the extra cream to make their ice cream. It was very bad winter driving that day with a lot of snow and slush on the road as Dick was leaving Ludington after delivering a load of cream. He was only a few miles out of Ludington when a car lost control and came across into Dick's lane, right in front of him! There was no time to try and avoid the car and they hit hard---resulting in three fatalities, a mother, infant daughter, and another man. Dick came through it with little harm. He only had a sore knee and some stiffness in his neck which bothered him yet the next day, but that was it. Again, a case of *angels* watching over Dick and God deciding it was not his time to come home to Heaven. What a traumatic time for Dick and us, but he got through that terrible time with the unmeasurable support of Christian friends and God's love. We all were shaken up and so sorry and distressed over the three who died. Three days after the tragedy, Dick went and talked to the mother of the lady who died, who also was the grandmother of the baby. He went to the funeral of two of the victims and met both families. They were glad he came. They did not blame Dick at all. Every year, until the last couple of years, we received a Christmas card from the grandmother, and we sent her one. But a tragedy like this goes beyond our understanding, and we easily wonder, "Why did this happen?" We do not have the answers but instead we need to have faith in God and trust in His plans, though it can be very difficult. Christians have the assurance of this verse in I Peter 5:7, "Casting all your care upon Him; for He careth for you" (KJV).

My frightening experience happened to me one summer evening, August 11, 2016. I wrote it all down after it happened and quote:

> God has a purpose for me yet on this earth and protected me last night! He had His *mighty angels* keep me safe! I had hurried out at 7 p.m. to mow the lawn in case it rained. First, I did a little in the back of the house and proceeded to our front lawn. I had JUST started my first lap around, going south along the sidewalk, when all of a sudden I heard this terrible, terrible loud noise! I thought, "Is it thunder? Or what could it possibly be?" I may have slowed down some; I do not know. But the next thing, I see all kinds of branches coming towards me! I fell right down! I do not know if a huge branch nudged me down; I do not recall anything hitting me. There were no scrapes on my arms or face from any branches. But somehow, I fell to the ground. There was no wind at all; the branch just fell, and I fell. I fell down, either from the force and *whoosh* of when it hit the ground, or my *guardian angel* pushed me out of the way. Either way, God certainly was protecting me that day! I

got right back up and started hearing voices . . . "Are you all right? Are you all right?" I did not know where the voices were coming from, but then I spotted two ladies by our driveway and on the other side of the HUGE branch. They saw it all happen when they were driving by and were worried sick about what had happened to me. Soon another couple also stopped by and kept asking if I was all right. They had been coming from the north and saw it all happen too. I have many pictures on my tablet to prove how close I was to the branch when it came down. I was about one and a half feet from where the huge part of the branch hit. My husband, Dick, figured just the force of that branch falling could have knocked me down. Later, I measured the branch, and it was 4 and a 1/2 feet around! I doubt if I would have been alive if I had taken one more step with the mower. The huge limb dropped from way up in the tree, close to 20 feet up. With such a big branch, from so high, there would have been a tremendous force when it hit the ground. I was so thankful that I was still alive!! There were all kinds of other branches on that huge branch---they blocked the whole road and cars could not get through.

Soon the police came and had someone cut up the branches to clear the road, since it was a main road. I did still finish cutting the middle of the lawn, and I felt okay doing it. But when I came in, I needed to sit. My legs were achy, my ears were sore or had pressure in them, my lower back started hurting---all probably the effects and shock of the trauma. I still felt shook up when I went to bed that night, but the next day I was fine. Dick had put some pictures on Facebook, so I had a lot of calls from family and friends the next day to make sure I was okay!

LITTLE ANGELS AND MIGHTY ANGELS

There were tons of large limbs to clean up off our yard, way more than what we as older people could take care of. Thankfully, the village hired someone to clean up the mess and take away the huge branch. Dick decided it was time to take the tree down. What would keep another huge branch like that one from falling on our house and wrecking it, or on the neighbor's house? This silver maple tree was in a tree pamphlet as the largest silver maple in two different counties. Years ago when the tree people measured the circumference of our maple for the brochure, it was 14 feet and 7 inches. When the tree was cut down in September of 2016, it measured 20 feet and 7 inches.

We hired a tree company from Rothbury (five miles away). They looked it over and accepted the job, though the owner of the company said it would be the largest tree they had ever taken down. It took the tree company four days to cut it all down, and it was just amazing to watch how they did it. Dick's sisters and brother-in-law often came and watched too, since it was really something to see. We could set our chairs up in a row in front of our garage and away from any danger. They even had to get a huge crane from Allendale one day (55 miles away) to help with the endeavor. This very big crane was capable of lifting the heavy trunk. One portion of the trunk alone was 13,000 pounds and the smaller portion about 5,000 pounds (the crane could weigh it). It was a good thing we decided to take the tree down, since they discovered quite a bit of rot in the center of the trunk. How many years would it have remained standing like that? At first it seemed empty without the tree, but now we do not mind it being gone . . . especially since I used to have to rake up at least 35 huge bags of leaves each year. As we sit at our kitchen table, we have much more visibility with the tree gone. The only thing we miss is how it very nicely shaded our large glassed-in front porch. Now our porch becomes way too hot during many days in the summer.

I have one more story to include that took place while working on this book. It certainly is another fitting story about *mighty angels* watching over God's children. On October 16, 2021, a large, very dangerous Haitian gang kidnapped 17 people who were on a two month mission trip in Haiti and held them hostage. The gang demanded a one million dollar ransom for each person, threatening to kill the hostages if their demands were not met. The group captured was made up of Mennonites, Amish, and conservative Anabaptists. They were abducted on their way home from the orphanage where they had helped out that day. Of the 17, there were five children, the youngest a baby of eight months, a three-year-old, six-year-old, 13-year-old, and a 15-year-old. Six (a mother and her five children) of those held captive were from Shelby, Michigan, only a few miles from where we live in New Era. The father had not gone with the group that morning because he stayed back to do some preparations for some classes he was instructing. This family belongs to the Hart Dunkard Brethren Church.

Many fervent prayers went up daily for this group by the community, local churches, and friends. The first two hostages were released in November, and three more on December 5. Then, what wonderful news when two of my daughters and I were making Christmas goodies in our kitchen, and my husband got a text on his phone that the abducted group was free! Dick was acquainted with this family and had visited with them a few times. It was later learned that they had made a daring escape. They had watched and planned for the right time and made their move during the night. They made it out through the unlocked side door, blocked on the outside with a boulder and fence post. They stuck a stick through a hole in the door to move the rock and fence post in order to make their escape while numerous guards were close by (in front of the building). The 12 men, women, and children then had to proceed through difficult, unfamiliar terrain with only the moonlight to help find their way. They walked on for about 7 or 8 miles through fields, through an area of terrible thorns and briars which made it so difficult to even find a way through, and they had to hike around a large lake. How frightened they had to be and worried that their kidnappers would again catch up with them! They walked until it began to get light and then they found someone who could help them. They were able to borrow a person's phone to call for help. How elated and thankful the husband and family's father, still in Haiti, had to be when he received word that they were free!

Praise God that no harm was done to this mission group physically though they did face hunger when receiving only small portions of food. Each day they had spaghetti in the morning and rice and a bean or meat sauce in the evening. They had been moved to a different camp for two weeks where they were able to have fresh fruit. For two months they wore their same clothing and were unable to wash their hair. The guys all ended up with beards since they had no way to shave.

But it was so helpful that they were able to encourage one another, since they were kept together as a group. So many people were rejoicing that this mother and her five children (as well as the rest of the group) were free and safely back in the states! It reminds us of the miraculous escape by the apostle Peter from prison as recorded in Acts 12:3-19. Peter was able to walk out of prison with an *angel* just like these twelve people were able to walk out with guards nearby .

For Peter too, people were praying. We read in verse five, "So Peter was kept in prison, but the church was EARNESTLY praying to God for him." In verse six and seven, "Peter was sleeping between two soldiers, bound with two chains, and sentries stood guard at the entrance. Suddenly an *angel* of the Lord appeared and a light shone in the cell. He struck [gently smote] Peter on the side and woke him up. 'Quick, get up!' he said, and the chains fell off Peter's wrists." This happened the night before Peter was to be executed. In verse eight the *angel* told Peter to follow him, so Peter followed him out of the prison. The story goes on that though Peter was heavily guarded, they passed the first and second guards. The guards never noticed them or the *angels* perhaps blinded them as they passed. I think the story of the group that was seized in Haiti sounds pretty similar . . . although many guards were close by, their *mighty angels* were right there with them, and God allowed them to get away. What a very miraculous escape for them! We give all the honor and praise to God for this miracle!

My husband and I were able to visit with them, and it was very meaningful and stirring to hear first hand their story of God's protection, love, and care! They expressed how God was with them in a mighty way and how Psalm 34:7 was so meaningful and relevant to all of this group, "The *angel* of the Lord encamps around those who fear Him, and He delivers them." They felt a circle of angels surrounding them while in captivity and during their escape.

There is a special story with the younger daughter who was fearful about trying to escape. But then she had a dream which brought a sense of peace the night they got away. She was sleeping a few hours before their escape at about 1 a.m. when she had the dream. In her dream she saw what she perceived in her eyes to be a *little angel*, or a little girl there with her. Then as they were making their escape, she felt the *little angel*, or little girl, take her hand and lead her into the brush. The little girl told her her name . . . it was the name of her sister who had died years ago due to a miscarriage! God provided this encouragement to her as they escaped! Though we often may not feel the presence of angels in our lives, this daughter did feel the presence of that little girl or *angel* right there beside her as they were walking the miles through difficult terrain and before they finally could call for help. I am sure there were angels right there beside these believers during their whole time of captivity and while making their escape.

What relief and great joy when 7:45 that morning there was loud pounding on the door at the mission, and they received word that the whole group was free and unharmed. Two vehicles were on their way to pick them up. It turned out they were only about 15 miles away from the mission base. By 3 p.m. that day they were on a plane provided by the FBI and on their way to Miami. What a true story of God's love and care for His people, about fervent prayers being answered, about many little miracles, and the presence of *angels* in believers' lives!

This concludes my many real life stories where God may have used His *mighty angels* to guide and protect us as Christians. Though this book will soon be finished, I am positive there will be many more instances in my life and the lives of others when I can see or feel *mighty angels* stepping in to shield us and intervene. I believe I have given you enough stories and Bible passages to back up why I believe in angels and in the God who created them, Who created you and me, and Who created all things. Knowing that our Heavenly Father provides these wonderful beings to serve us and to take care of us makes me feel more thankful to Him and closer to Him! I confess before I started writing this book about angels, I did not often think about these heavenly beings. I believe now with the verses pertaining to angels and some real-to-life stories, I will be more conscious of them and this is a good thing. We may not always be aware of all the *mighty angels* in our lives, but there will come a day when we can know the full extent of angels in our lives, as well as many other miraculous things. I Corinthians 13:12 states, "Now we see but a poor reflection as in a mirror; then we shall see face to face. Now I know in part; then I shall know fully, even as I am fully known." Or in the Living New Testament paraphrase it reads, "We can see and understand only a little about God now, as if we were peering at His reflection in a poor mirror; but someday we are going to see Him in His completeness, face to face. Now all that I know is hazy and blurred, but then I will see everything clearly, just as clearly as God sees into my heart right now." So then we will see everything VERY clearly and understand all about angels also.

Yes, I definitely believe in angels! I hope with some of my stories in this book, you too will start believing in angels if you do not already. I have read of those who because of an accident or illness were on their deathbed and have felt the presence of an angel in their room. Again, how very special that God created these wondrous and marvelous spirit beings to serve and help us while we are on this earth. Angels are everything good---pure, messengers, beings of light, radiant, faithful to God, and servants. But I need to state along with these good angels are the fallen angels who are servants of Satan. While God's angels are serving as protectors, helpers, and everything good, Satan's angels are doing everything bad and trying to win the war of stealing souls for Satan. There is a raging battle going on every day between the good angels and the bad angels that we often do not even think about. Make sure your soul is safe in the arms of Jesus so that you can be with Him in Heaven some day. And make your decision for Christ today, before it is too late! You never know what tomorrow may bring or if you even have another day left on this earth! We have turmoil in our world going on right now with the Ukraine and Russian conflict. What repercussions may happen because of this battle? There could be serious consequences throughout the world in the weeks and months ahead. Or just this past week a teenage boy from the community was killed in an unfortunate car accident. We just never know what may happen or when it may occur! We need to be ready!

God has never promised that our walk in life will be free of problems and difficulties---that our path will always be smooth and safe. But we have to remember Psalm 121:1-2 where it states, "I lift up my eyes to the hills---where does my help come from? My help comes from the Lord, the Maker of Heaven and earth." Also, we read in Psalm 90:12, "Teach us to number our days and recognize how few they are; help us to spend them as we should." (Liv. Bible). Take time to enjoy your families and friends; life on this earth is so very short. Take time today to list some unexpected blessings. I wrote the following blessings down once: "For me today it is the warmth and beauty of summertime, for two boys helping edge our lawn for us as we get older, the good smell of squash in the air from the canning company close by, for emails from my daughters, for the health of our grandchildren, for the beautiful white clouds floating against the bright blue sky, for God's love to each one of us, and for my opportunity to write a book."

My two oldest grandchildren attended a retreat in Denver, Colorado with other young people from their church. They learned practical ways to share the Good News about Jesus and then went to downtown Denver to put it in practice. It was a real growing experience for them in witnessing to others, and was beneficial to those they talked to. They used the opportunities they were given to talk to others, and we too ought to be mindful of the opportunities God gives us. We as Christians need to be fruitful. I am reminded of Galatians 5:22-23, and as Christians we need to practice the fruit of the Spirit which are, "Love, joy, peace, patience, kindness, goodness, faithfulness, gentleness and self-control." May we always avail ourselves of every opportunity to help impart these fruits to our loved ones, to our neighbors, to our friends, and to the unsaved. The world could become a better place if more people would show more love, kindness, goodness, patience, and gentleness in a manner that is humble and meek. We need to be attentive to the leading of the Holy Spirit as he directs us to opportunities to serve God. In our retirement we cannot do too much resting and not any serving. We need to have empathy for those in need. Let us all try harder and ask the Lord to help us each day! It is so easy to become bogged down in the busyness and in the circumstances of life. We need to change our perspective and look upward to God for His help and encouragement instead of focusing on ourselves and the problems, difficulties, and hardships of life. If we are faithful in doing the small things and perform them well, God will bless us for it and give us greater gifts and responsibilities. And to think . . . each new day is clean and we can have a fresh start filled with opportunities to be used by God. Each morning we should start the day thanking God for the gift of a brand-new day and the numerous possibilities to serve Him. I remember a speaker once who emphasized over and over that our main purpose in life is to be a witness, to tell others about the Lord Jesus Christ.

Another new chapter my husband and I have now entered is our retirement years. I found this quote by Vance Havner, "The last chapter in life can be the best." What I have witnessed thus far in my retirement years, it makes me feel that could be so. I wrote earlier how free I felt when I stopped driving school bus after 25 years. I even made some notations about when I was feeling especially happy with my new freedoms (2/28/14) and quote:

> Just a quick note again to say I am so enjoying my "Golden Years." To wake up in the morning and be able to choose whether or not to stay in bed a bit longer . . . and I lie there thinking, "This is the life!" Usually I do not sleep in that much because I am eager to get going on whatever I wish to do. I can get up, and I do not need to rush around to drive the bus; I can work on the many projects I have to do around the house. I enjoy life!

I feel at peace and feel contentment. Not that I did not enjoy life in my busier years, but now I have the time to appreciate and relish it. I hope my face shows that to others; we read in Proverbs 15:13, "A happy heart makes the face cheerful!"

I like my Mondays through Fridays the best because weekends tend to become busier. My days and weeks still fly by! I wonder . . . how is it that when we now have more free time, and we do not need to rush around so much as we did in earlier years, that still time goes so very quickly! I feel a bit sad about that and regretful. This thought is mentioned in the latter part of Psalm 39:4, ". . . How fleeting is my life." Also, in verse five of that same chapter, "Each man's life is but a breath." That certainly is how I often feel - - - my life is but a breath when time keeps passing so quickly! But I'm getting some overdue projects done, and I am doing fun things too like watching tennis, playing pickleball, and reading. Being retired makes me happy and free as a bird!

Later I wrote:

I am writing again about my totally enjoyable retired life. My husband says, "Don't you get bored at home?" And I say "never." I always find things to do; I believe I have enough projects in mind to keep me busy for ten more years! I so love the freedom of doing whatever I please and whenever I please. First, I may have felt a bit guilty when I retired and was not being as productive each and every day. Now I figure as long as I am over all getting something constructive accomplished each week, it's okay! It is okay to take a vacation day now and then, like today I watched a couple inspiring movies on TV and snowmobiled. After all, I worked pretty hard when growing up picking asparagus, cherries, planting trees, weeding trees, garden work, mowing lawns, helping Dad on the farm, and doing hard physical work. Later, I married, and I had a very busy life with four girls close together in age, and even added driving bus to that. Now it is time to slow down and "Smell the Roses." I may not even have ten years left, and I want to enjoy what God has blessed us with---good health, a comfortable home, a good church, a wonderful family, and the beauty of God's creation. I worked and hustled and bustled in life for about 60 years. It is time to put up my feet and be happy me. But I also want to serve the Lord and be attentive to the opportunities that He puts before me.

We should not become discouraged or complain as we get up in years, even though we may find our bodies plainly do not work as well anymore. We probably find that we do less and less; we cannot do nearly as much as we once did. We should never think, however, that our lives no longer have meaning or purpose. Maybe we will have physical limitations when we get up in age, but we can always pray for others, be encouraging, have a good listening ear, be kind and caring, and challenge others to live as Christians and do what is right! I often use the motto, "It is the right thing to do." During what may well be the last days for some of us, thank God He is still right beside us leading and guiding all the way! We attended a funeral today of a lady who lived to be 96 years old, and they referred to her as a matriarch because she was wise and dignified. She also lived her life as a role model to others, and she was generous, kind, thoughtful, caring, always striving to live for her family and for others. The pastor said she finished well, and that should be our goal also. We hope and pray that when we walk through Heaven's gates, when Christ meets us He will say, "Well done you good and faithful servant!"

I hope we can say along with Paul in Philippians 4:11, "I have learned, in whatever state I am, to be content" (K.J.V.). I do feel contentment in my retirement years. The Bible is full of stories of people who God used in their later (retirement) years. Though we slow down and may face frustrations and challenges in our old age, we should not give up but hang in there. These golden years can still be pleasing, satisfying, enriching, gratifying, and inspiring. Who knows? Maybe these times can be the best years yet!

As we are nearing our Heavenly home, it is time to recap and think about the past. Have we been faithful to God? Are we on the right path . . . the path that leads us to God? Are we continuing to be faithful? Are we willing to follow where He leads? Our children and grandchildren are watching us and are following us. Are we leading them in the best possible way? Are we following Christ's footsteps so others will follow His steps also? At the age we are now, we can still be a help to our grandchildren by being interested in their activities, keeping in touch with them, praying often for them, listening to them, and by being good examples.

Life gets more difficult as we get older but there are benefits too. We are free from all the responsibilities we once had, we have more hours for family and friends, we can have the fun of enjoying the little things and special joys in life, and we can spend more time in God's Word and in prayer.

Retirement allows us to pursue some other interests, hobbies, and new pastimes. For me, during the last several years, I have included something new . . . authoring two books, something I never dreamed possible! I feel that was a positive accomplishment and hopefully those who read the books may learn something, be inspired, and find them enjoyable reading. If so, my work will not have been in vain. In your golden years, find some fulfilling and productive projects to do. We do not want this to be true of us from Ecclesiastes 2:11, "Yet when I surveyed all that my hands had done and what I had toiled to achieve, everything was meaningless, a chasing after the wind; nothing was gained under the sun." It goes on to say in chapter 3:12, "I know that there is nothing better for men than to be happy and do good while they live." I believe that can apply to our retirement years also . . . "To be happy and do good."

On 2/26/17, I wrote this paragraph about retirement and I quote:

> This is the fourth year of my bus retirement. I was just thinking I need to write again how much I enjoy being retired! I say every day is a weekend for me--- since weekends you can sleep later and do special things, and now I can do that ALL WEEK LONG! I so enjoy my freedoms, I enjoy my home, I enjoy life! Dick often uses the phrase also and says, "He enjoys life!" I enjoy getting projects done that I have wanted to do for years, appreciate having less stress in my life, and I feel content and happy in the place God has for me now. I look forward to my days, my plans, my goals. I know how busy I used to be raising my family. I think it is okay to take some rest times from all our labor in our "Golden Years."

As I get older, it is hard to admit but my body is getting a bit worn out, I move about slower, and sometimes I am tired; so I feel on those days it is okay to take it a little easier. Then on the days when I feel more energetic, I can get things done. Over the years when our children were in Christian schools, it required so much volunteer work which we needed to do to help with the costs of Christian education. I also did hours and hours of extra volunteer time that came with driving the bus for 23 years for our Christian school, as well as many other things. Finally, I just got to the point of feeling "burned out." So now I look forward to my retirement days and to have a better balance between being too busy and relaxing. I thank God for my feelings of happiness and peace these days, and may Dick and I continue in good health and strength to be able to enjoy each other and to enjoy life!

God exemplified the importance of rest. In Genesis 2:2 we read, "By the seventh day God had finished the work He had been doing; so on the seventh day He rested from all His work." I feel too in our latter years once our work is about done, we can rest and take it more easy. God rested when He finished His work. Once we have retired from a job it is okay to rest from our labors. God established the importance of a day of rest each week. He also has given us nights to rest. When you go to sleep at night, rest knowing you have accomplished something worthwhile that day. That gives you fulfillment and satisfaction. I read once "It is sad to grow old but nice to ripen" (Bardot). Being retired is a time to think back, reminisce, and remember about the "good ol' days." There are many things for me to do yet . . . projects, reading, playing pickleball, emailing, yard work and gardening, housework, biking, and helping others. Being happy, glad, pleased, delighted, joyous, content, satisfied, and cheerful describes my retirement. My husband is mostly retired and enjoys it when the weather is nice. He often works at a friend's place a mile down the road repairing tractors, getting them running to sell and doing other mechanical work. He enjoys that so it is more like a hobby to him. Dick is also involved with the local tractor club in the area. He enjoys the beautiful weather from spring through fall doing lots of things outdoors. Winter time is a bit more of a problem and a challenge for him, since he cannot find as much to do, and he really does not like the cold weather. It makes it difficult for him as he is not a person that wants to sit around much . . . he always likes to be on the go! I am almost two years older than Dick and that age difference never has mattered over the years. Lately though, Dick still likes to go, go, and this often includes me. Most of the time this is okay, but other times, I would rather do something a bit more relaxing around our home which I enjoy very much. My roots go very deep at this house in New Era where I have lived most of my life. I used to feel a close bond to the farmhouse in which I grew up. Now the memories are at this house with my husband and our daughters. My roots go so deep here that it would be very hard to transplant me!

I seem to be including quite a bit about the retirement years. There are some Bible verses I would like to quote; first, from Proverbs 16:31, "Gray hair is a crown of splendor; it is attained by a righteous life." I think that is a nice way of explaining gray hair! What a wonderful promise in Isaiah 46:4, "I will be your God through all your lifetime, yes, even when your hair is white with age. I made you and I will care for you. I will carry you along and be your Savior" (Liv. Bible). And in Psalm 90:12, "Teach us to number our days and recognize how few they are; help us to spend them as we should" (Liv. Bible). Quoting directly from my devotional booklet I wrote:

> It was rather a strange thing last night and I thought about it a few times throughout the day and now again . . . I remember lying in bed awake for a while during the night and thinking: I am almost 60 years old (back in 2002). How can this be? I feel like I am the same Judy Kuipers Walhout from long ago encased in this growing old body. I do not really feel I should be this old! And I don't want to be so old - - - 30 or 40 would be all right! Maybe though, God willing, I will have 20 years left but that seems like a "drop in the bucket." Sometimes, I wish I could do it all over again - - - learn from my many mistakes, and do it so much better the next time around. So with those thoughts I would advise those of you who are younger parents reading this . . . listen, you won't have forever! Make the most of every opportunity now! You also will be 60 before you know it! (And now I am 77 already!) And for myself, all I can say is God please forgive me for all the times I have failed and those times are like the grains of sand on the shore. Forgive us, comfort us, and help us look forward and not behind! Help Your great love to encompass us so that we feel important and of value and not like failures. Yes, we need to remember life on this earth is short. In Psalm 90:10 we read, "The days of our years are threescore years and ten; and if by reason of strength they be fourscore years . . . " (KJV). A score is 20 years and that makes me past that 70 year mark already! Thus, I consider each new day a gift from God, or a bonus day! I will include this little poem:

"The clock of life is wound but once,

And no man has the power

To tell just when the hands will stop,

At late or early hour.

To lose one's wealth is sad indeed,

To lose one's health is more;

To lose one's soul is such a loss

That no man can restore." (Anonymous.)

When we think that our life could soon be over on this earth, we refer to Hebrews 13:14 which says, "For this world is not our home; we are looking forward to our everlasting home in Heaven" (Living N.T). And the beautiful song that is so fitting says, "When all my labors and trials are over, and I am safe on that beautiful shore. Just to be near the dear Lord I adore, will through the ages be glory for me. And when by His grace I shall look on His face. That will be glory for me."

To make the most of our "bonus days," we should be happy, full of fun, caring and loving to others. Another thing to remember is in Proverbs 16:1, "We can make our plans, but the final outcome is in God's hands" (Liv. Bible). We do not have to participate in all the hurry and busyness much anymore, and we can find abounding rest and peace. For me personally with my extra time, I found fulfillment, satisfaction, and happiness with the task of authoring two books. Each book took right around a year to write, edit, and publish. I have a new respect for authors knowing how much work is involved, the many challenges there are to face, and how many countless hours and days it takes to write a book. This second book is much longer than my first book, and I worked pretty steadily on it for days, weeks, months, and over a year. Often I would think there was no end in sight. I would not have had time to do this during my bus driving years and when busy raising our girls. But this was a way to use my time wisely and not waste some of my latter years. I wanted to record my memories in a book but hopefully, and far more importantly, I want to touch someone's life and steer them towards God! I also found by sharing and reflecting on stories, thoughts, scripture verses, spiritual insight, and what was important to me that it was beneficial for me too, and I felt drawn closer to God. What a special gift and reward for me!

You may be thinking . . . that is it. Retirement is our final chapter in life. But this is not true; it is not the final chapter! The final chapter is when we get to Heaven! And that chapter will go on forever! We need to be ready and prepared since we read in I Thessalonians 5:2, "For you know very well that the day of the Lord will come like a thief in the night." This will be Christ's second coming, and the trumpet shall sound when He comes again. It will be dramatic, sudden, and unexpected. Also, God's children may have an *angel* alongside them when they meet God face to face. Luke 16:22 says, "The time came when the beggar died and the *angels* carried him to Abraham's side [which would be Heaven]." I have read a couple Bible scholars' views on this verse also, and they feel Christians will be escorted by *angels* to Heaven. I find that thought very awesome and comforting! To me, it is not quite as scary to face death when it comes knocking on the door knowing one of God's *mighty angels* might accompany me. There is a future in Heaven for those who have accepted the plan of salvation through Christ's redeeming blood, and sadly a future in Hell for those who have rejected Christ and His promises found in God's Word.

A last thought for those who at this very time may be experiencing sorrow, heartaches, pain, depression, worry, grief, and unhappiness---and we all have these things at one time or another as we walk down life's paths. There is a solution and an answer, and that is by leaning on Christ. He is a strong friend that will never leave or forsake you. When the loads and burdens are too hard to bear, He will help carry us through the troubled times. You cannot find help in a world that is full of unrest, uncertainty, deceitfulness, and corruption. None of the world's things are lasting, and they do not bring real joy, peace, happiness, or contentment. Only Christ, if we believe in Him, gives us true joy, peace, and happiness! And Christians should show this happiness by being joyful, enthusiastic, and wear a smile. We had a guest pastor recently who mentioned using your *"Face Praise."* I like that idea. We are never too old to praise God with our facial expressions. We may be able to raise someone's spirits, just by giving them a nice smile. A good quote, "Smiling is happy and fun and feels good, looks nice, and does not cost anything." It is so much better if we go around with a smile on our face rather than looking gloomy and sad. May we be eager and willing to praise the Lord and have joy in living . . . even in our later years!

Another asset in life is to add a little humor. My mom was very good at that. I wrote this in my devotional book:

> Sometimes we forget something or do something a bit odd and right away we are labeled as someone "losing it." A few examples of late: 1. I went to town

with a daughter with two different, mismatched shoes on . . . thankfully, I did not have to get out of the car. I did not notice my error until we returned home! 2. I cut an apple in quarters and thought what a hard apple . . . until I noticed I was trying to cut with the dull side of the knife! 3. I "mistakenly" poured liquid Spic and Span in the washing machine instead of liquid Tide—hmmm! So my response to these incidents . . . humor. They really perked up my day with the funniness of the three situations. So if we can see the humor in our mistakes and get a kick out of it, then all is well. If you are happy, carefree, joyful, buoyant, merry, and content, then your whole day often can go so much better. No matter what you are facing, a smile can only make it better. Life is too short to spend it being angry, bored, or gloomy.

Going on to another thought is a prayer I read that said, "Dear God, we need help each day to control the thorns, weeds, and diseases that are trying to choke us out and stunt our growth in You, O Lord. We need You in these battles of life so we can grow and bear fruit to glorify You. Do not allow our feet to be planted in shallow ground but instead in deep and fertile soil so with Your tender care, we can grow and mature into healthy, fit plants--- flourishing in fruits and accomplishments for You. Amen."

One more project I was thinking we should be working on in our retirement years is "getting our houses in order." We do not know how many more "bonus days" God will give us on this earth. We enjoy our families, our friends, our homes, being retired, the change of seasons, trips, seeing new things, and enjoy God's creation to list a few. I admit I feel bad and sad about having to leave it all when God calls me home. That is understandable, I think, for most people when only seeing it from the human point of view. But someone said, "You ain't seen anything yet!" He meant nothing here on this earth can compare to what is ahead in Heaven. Imagine a place where there will be no fighting, no arguing, no anger, no sorrow, no illness or hurts, no more pain, no heartaches, no burdens, no sin, or no darkness---that place will be Heaven! Think of things you really love and enjoy, the very best fun times you have ever experienced, and some of your happiest moments and special times . . . in Heaven they will be hundreds of times more exciting, fulfilling, happy, and wonderful! Our human minds cannot even begin to comprehend what it will be like! And it will be for all eternity . . . never-ending! So yes, put your physical house in order by sorting your keepsakes (and junk), get rid of a lot of the "stuff" so you do not leave it for your children to do, and really "clean house." More importantly though, we need to have our "spiritual house" in order, meaning you as a person (and me). Make sure you believe in Jesus as your Savior, attend a Bible believing church each Sunday, read your Bible and pray, and live each day for Christ. Then you will be prepared and have both of your houses in order! My next project after this book is completed is to do that very thing . . . get my two houses in order. I feel at the age we are in this chapter of our lives, we are likely nearing our Heavenly home. We are on the home stretch and we should have our affairs in order. If the "home stretch" seems a bit scary, think of the words of the song that says that we need to turn our eyes upon Jesus and look to Him and His wonderful face. Then the things of earth will grow gradually dim in the light of His glory and grace.

And when the infirmities of old age start limiting and bothering you, try to focus your eyes upwards and look steadfastly ahead to what God has promised in Heaven. It is God's plan, it is His will, and the best is yet to come! I like to summarize those last thoughts in six words, and I often repeat them in my mind. "God's Plan; God's Will; Rest Assured!" When doubts assail you, hardships and sorrows come (and they will), and your life seems full of troubles, repeat those six words over and over again. Leave it all in God's hands; it is the only way to find peace!

God loves us and gives His love freely to mankind. Our job is to reflect this love to others; and we need to be sensitive to the needs of others. I decided there is no better way to conclude than to quote the verse about how broad, mammoth, immense, and vast is the love of God. Nothing can compare to the love of God! Even the sky that appears to go on forever and ever, or the stars that are too numerous to count cannot at all compare to the immense love of God. Romans 8:38-39 (KJV) tells about this love, "For I am persuaded [convinced], that neither death, nor life, nor angels, nor principalities [demons], nor powers, nor things present, nor things to come, nor height, nor depth, nor any other creature [or anything else in all creation], shall be able to separate us from the love of God, which is in Christ Jesus our Lord!"

In our days ahead that are left on this earth, this should be our intent, "Strip off anything that slows us down or holds us back, and especially those sins that wrap themselves so tightly around our feet and trip us up; and let us run with patience the particular race that God has set before us" (Heb. 12:1 Living N.T.). Or another wording, "Let us run with perseverance the race marked out for us" (NIV). To run with "perseverance" means we must patiently and steadfastly continue on towards heaven as our goal with total determination and endurance! And when this race is finished, "He [God] will wipe every tear from their eyes. There will be no more death or mourning or crying or pain, for the old order of things has passed away" (Rev. 21:4). What amazing, astounding, breathtaking and marvelous rewards God has promised everyone and anyone who is on the right road, navigating down God's path in this world! I encourage and urge you all to keep on the important narrow path and may God through His *mighty angels* keep you from veering to the right or left or from stumbling or falling! Let us diligently run the race God has set before us, and by faith and His grace and His strength let us not grow weary!

It is my sincere hope and prayer that all of you who have finished reading *Little Angels and Mighty Angels* enjoyed, valued, and appreciated it . . . even as much as I have enjoyed, taken pleasure in, and earnestly and lovingly wrote it. Thank you, my readers, from all my heart! May God bless and keep you! Amen and Amen!

Judy's 1964 Chevy Impala with Car Top Carrier

Our Apartment's Pool

Coxes, our California Family

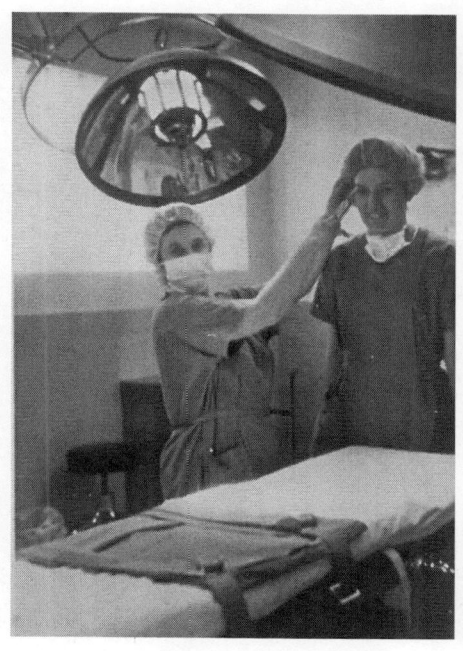

Judy (on right) at Work

California's Beautiful Palm Trees

Cam in the Snow on the Mountains

Judy's Dad, Aunt Emma, Mom, and Judy at Knotts Berry Farm

Dick & Judy's Wedding, 1973

Our Girls by the Red Fence Judy Built

Riding our Solex Bikes

Back Yard Beauty in the Wintertime

Clumps of Snow on the Branches

Dick & Judy Ready for Snowmobiling Fun

Judy Enjoying Winter Beauty

Our Four Daughters

*Grandparents (with Alicia), Henry Walhout,
Clarence & Elsie Kuipers, Ethel Walhout*

Tree House Judy Built

Girls each had their Own Garden Plots

Fun Times with the '35 Plymouth

Our Four Girls and the Dogs, Trixie & Rocky

255

Nichole Shoveling Snow off the Roof

Two of Dick's Sharp Restored Tractors

Judy's Gnome House, Waterfall, Creek, and Pond

Dick and Judy with all their Grandchildren by Mackinac Bridge

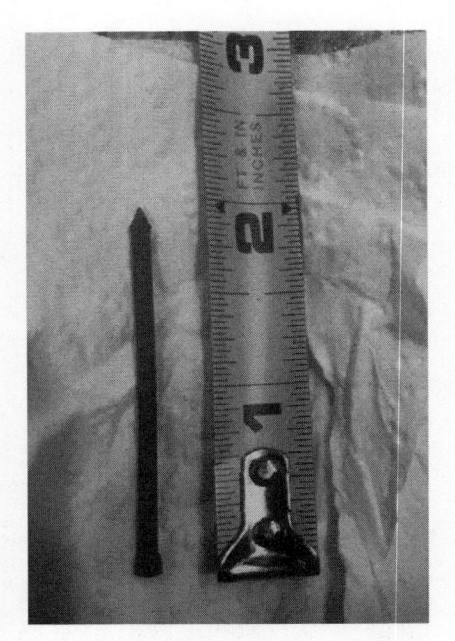

Randy's Swallowed Two Inch Nail

Reuben with some of his Planes

Tiny David, Born at Two Pounds Eleven and a Half Ounces

Dick with Grandkids

Dick with Grandkids

Judy with Grandson, David

Dick & Judy by their Huge Silver Maple Tree

Judy's Close Call with this Huge Branch

Look how big the Maple Tree was

Judy Standing by the Cut Down Trunk

Dick & Judy's Home in New Era

Dick and Judy

A NOTE FROM THE AUTHOR

2020 will be remembered by me since it was the year I wrote my first book, *A Farm Girl's Memories*. When I sent in my manuscript it was a huge day for me! I wrote down that "I am feeling elated, relieved, satisfied, a bit nervous and anxious about how it will be accepted by the publisher. I put in so many hours these last several weeks to get it fine-tuned and ready to go. I am in somewhat of a daze thinking I actually did it . . . I wrote a book!" It was something I never dreamed possible. Here I am two years later and looking forward to when I complete my new book and send the finished manuscript in for publishing.

For those of you who have authored a book, I'm sure you feel as I do . . . it is very hard to come to the end of the story and to end the book. I have shared a lot of my life's story, but certainly not all of it. I have shared some ideas and some advice, and I have tried to share scripture and thoughts about the love and sovereignty of God. I have shared some things touching and very important to me about my husband, my children, and my grandchildren. My heart's prayer is that I presented the stories and material in such a way that others will enjoy and delight in reading the book, and it interests them enough so that they will have a hard time putting it down. This title of "author" is very new to me, being this is only the second book I have written. I feel somewhat inadequate and humbled to even accept that title, but I guess if I publish two books, the title is justified. As with my first book, it is a very rewarding, gratifying, satisfying, enriching, pleasing, and fulfilling experience to finish a book, and hopefully, this one will be published in the year 2022, two years after my first book.

Since I had numerous requests for another book, I hope this book will be interesting, stirring, and inspiring to those who asked for a second book. To my sister's friends in California who requested a second book, I hope you will not be disappointed! The book came together well, and I feel really good about it! I feel with God's help I have done my best, and I gave it my all knowing it may be my last book. I do not have enough stories and material for another. I never could see myself writing a book, but now that I have attempted it, I enjoy doing it very much even though it is very time consuming and takes a huge amount of work and effort! But I feel it is time very well spent. What better legacy to pass down to my family and friends than a book that I have authored and put my heart into. Also, it was a chance to tell individuals how important it is to turn their lives over to Christ before it is too late.

Sadly, I will have to come to an end which is very difficult. As I mentioned in my first book, it feels like I am saying good-bye to a very good friend. Each book took right around a year to write, edit, and get published. There were so many days, weeks, and months when I dedicated each day and evening to working on the book. It took a lot of time, effort, motivation, mental energy, and patience to write it. It was exciting for me again when my second book started to develop and emerge with me working on it earnestly and steadily.

Thank you for choosing *Little Angels and Mighty Angels,* and I pray that it held your attention. It was not hard for me to come up with a title for the book when I began to reflect on the many events and happenings over the years where I could see God providing His watchcare, protection, and service through His *mighty angels.* I hope too in some small way it may have brought you closer to God, or maybe made you more determined to spread the seeds to help further Christ's Kingdom. I would love to hear from you and how you felt about the book. You can email me at tennisjaw@gmail.com. May God bless you and provide you with protection and care from His *mighty angels* as you walk down the various paths in your life's journey. These paths may be crooked, filled with obstacles, uneven and full of big bumps. Sometimes we have to turn around and go a different way, but for Christians God and His *mighty angels* are right there alongside us guiding and protecting each step of the way!